PRAYERS AND AIDS FOR PUBLIC WORSHIP

William Powell Tuck

Energion Publications
Cantonment, Florida
2025

Advance Praise for Prayers and Aids for Public Worship

This book is a treasure! Drawing on his decades of experience as a pastor, Bill Tuck has crafted these prayers, litanies, affirmations, and benedictions with such heart and tenderness that he is able to express the joys and sorrows that we each bring to worship each week. He also speaks to the special, yet occasional, worship services that sometimes get overlooked (Commencement, Communion prayers, or those times simply when our hearts are "in a storm"). As I read and pray Bill's imaginative and inspired prayers and litanies, my own creativity in worship preparation has been encouraged time and again. Yours will too.

Dr. Daniel Glaze
Pastor, River Road Church, Baptist, Richmond, Virginia

I know of no similar work that I could endorse with such enthusiasm, but I heartily recommend this stellar collection as the best you will find. Faithfully employed, these prayers and meditative responses will enrich your worship ministry.

Dr. John Killinger
(See his Introduction to this book.)

Reading through this resource of worship aids brought an immediate reaction: this would have been invaluable in my years of pastoral ministry, and I will make certain my pastor gets a copy. Each subject (calls to worship, invocations, pastoral prayers, etc.) is preceded by a brief introduction explaining the what and why for use in worship. Each chapter reflects depth, insight, and the perfect blending of mind and heart. All the material is life related and faith directed.

I also realized that the calls to worship, invocations, and pastoral prayers can be used now in my morning devotional time. The benedictions will make excellent closures for this time. I cannot think of a better way to conclude than with this benediction: "May you sense God beside you to comfort you. God behind you to encourage you. God beneath you to support you. God before you to guide you. God above you to sharpen your vision. And most of all God within you to assure you of divine grace and love." Amen. (p. 69).

Any worship service will be enriched, and the congregation will be blessed by the use of resources found in this treasury. My suggestion: buy this book and begin immediately to receive its blessings.

Ronald Higdon
Pastor emeritus of Broadway Baptist Church, Louisville, KY.
Author of *Faith Never Stands Alone* and other books.

Those of us who proclaim the gospel on a regular basis know how much we benefit not just from disciplined and prayerful study but from resources that stretch our thinking and focus, even our choice of words and images. The same can be said of our development of prayers and liturgy which contribute to worship experience at least as much as sermons. In his latest book, Prayers and Aids for Public Worship, Bill Tuck has provided just such a resource, a marvelous collection of liturgies and prayers informed by the deep reservoir of his personal experience as a pastor and professor. Some of these we may use, others will shape our thinking, all will enrich the worship life of the congregations we are privileged to serve. With each new book he writes, a larger audience benefits from the warmth and wisdom those of us who have known Dr. Tuck as mentor and friend have come to cherish.

Christopher C. F. Chapman
Pastor, First Baptist Church, Raleigh

Other Books By
William Powell Tuck

+ Facing Grief and Death: Living with Dying
+ The Way for All Seasons: The Beatitudes for the 21st Century
+ The Compelling Faces of Jesus
+ The Modem Shapers of Baptist Thought in America
+ The Journey to the Undiscovered Country: What's Beyond Death
+ The Last Words from the Cross
+ The Church Under the Cross
+ The Lord's Prayer Today
+ A Pastor Preaching: Toward a Theology of the Proclaimed Word
+ The Church in Today's World
+ The Ten Commandments: Their Meaning Today
+ The Left Behind Fantasy: The Theology Behind the Left Behind Tales
+ Christmas Is for the Young: Whatever Their Age
+ Through the Eyes of a Child
+ The Struggle for Meaning (editor)
+ Lessons from Old Testament Characters
+ Jesus' Journey to the Cross

+ Conversations with My Grandchildren about God, Religion, and Life

+ Markings Along the Way: The Signs of Jesus in the Gospel of John

+ Star Thrower: A Pastor's Handbook

+ Holidays, Holy Days, and Special Days

+ A Positive Word for Christian Lamenting: Funeral Homilies

+ The Forgotten Beatitudes: Worshipping Through Stewardship

+ The Abiding Presence: Communion Meditations

+ Which Voice Will You Follow?

+ The Difficult Sayings of Jesus

+ The Rebirth of the Church

+ A Pastoral Prophet: Sermons and Prayers of Wayne Oates (editor)

+ The Pulpit Ministry of the Pastors of River Road Church, Baptist (editor)

+ The Bible as Our Guide for Spiritual Growth (editor)

+ Ministry: An Ecumenical Challenge (editor)

+ Knowing God: Religious Knowledge in the Theology of John Baillie

+ Overcoming Sermon Block: The Preacher's Workshop

+ Beginning and Ending a Pastorate

+ A Revolutionary Gospel: Salvation in the Theology of Walter Rauschenbusch

+ Authentic Evangelism: Sharing the Good News with Sense And Sensitivity

+ Getting Past the Pain: Making Sense of Life's Darkness

About the Author

William Powell Tuck, a native of Virginia, has served as a pastor, seminary professor, college professor, interim pastor, and intentional interim pastor. He is the author of more than forty books including Challenges for Today's Living and The Rebirth of the Church. He has received a Doctor of Divinity degree from the University of Richmond, in 1999 he received the Medallion Award from the national Boys and Girls Club of America, in 1997 The Pastor of the Year Award from the Academy of Parish Clergy, in 2016 received the Wayne Oates Award from the Oates Institute in Louisville, Kentucky, and in 2024 received Bluefield University Hall of Distinguished Graduates Award. He and his wife, Emily, are the parents of two children and five grandchildren, and live in Richmond, Virginia.

PRAYERS AND AIDS FOR PUBLIC WORSHIP

WILLIAM POWELL TUCK

Energion Publications
Cantonment, Florida
2025

ISBN: 978-1-63199-931-4
eISBN: 978-1-63199-932-1

Energion Publications
1241 Conference Rd
Cantonment, FL 32533

pubs@energion.com
energion.com

In
Memory and appreciation
Of
Joann Feazell
Minister of Music & Organist
At
First Baptist Church, Bristol, Virginia
For over forty years
And with whom
I had the privilege.
Of
Planning weekly worship
And
Knowing her as a friend

TABLE OF CONTENTS

INTRODUCTION

Every minister I know has a very crowded schedule and wants to turn in a quality performance with everything on it. One of the real "biggies" on his or her list every week is the preparation of prayers and responses for the Sunday worship bulletin. These can be very time-consuming, as any minister knows. When I was a pastor, I tried to set aside at least one day a week to devote to this demanding task.

I would have given an eye-tooth or two for a book like this one, but unfortunately, I did not have that option. I remember laboring every week of my ministry to create the very best array of prayers and responses I could possibly assemble. I know, had this book been available then, that I would have leaned heavily on it, because William Tuck was a faithful and articulate composer of such materials, and I would have relished the opportunity to employ those materials in the services I was planning.

For many years Tuck was a very successful pastor, and hundreds of people flocked to the St. Matthews Baptist Church, Louisville, Kentucky, every Sunday because they respected his work and knew they would leave his service each time with a sense of having truly been in the presence of God and had their lives touched again by the often-elusive holiness of the Almighty. They knew their pastor would have spread the very best meal possible for them.

Bill and I have been friends for many years, and I know the depth of dedication and meaningfulness that has characterized his ministry through all that time. Even a casual browser in this book will instantly recognize its worth and give thanks to God for the remarkable character and personal devotion of its creator.

I know of no similar work that I could endorse with such enthusiasm, but I heartily recommend this stellar collection as the best you will find. Faithfully employed, these prayers and meditative responses will enrich your worship ministry beyond all imagining and bring to your own congregation each week at least some of the very special quality that marked Bill Tuck's own pastoral leadership for many years!

John Killinger

(Former professor, Vanderbilt Divinity School, former pastor of First Congregational Church of Los Angeles, and author of *Fundamentals of Preaching*, and many other books.)

PREFACE

A lot of a pastor's worship preparation involves various prayers. I do not believe that a pastor's prayers should be merely spontaneous or an impromptu moment delivery. They should be carefully planned and reflect the focus of the worship for that day. Sermon professors have suggested that a pastor should spend at least an hour for each minute one preaches. That would mean that a twenty-minute sermon should require twenty hours of preparation. I believe the same model should be observed for the preparation of pastoral prayers.

All of the prayers and worship aids for a worship service should cause the pastor to plan and carefully reflect the Invocation, offertory, pastoral prayer, the prayer after the sermon, and the benediction as well as the Call to Worship and any Affirmation of Faith used in the service. It was my practice in several of my churches to share copies of my sermons with my congregation the next Sunday following when I preached it. I also included my pastoral prayer with the sermon. I often received favorable comments from parishioners on my prayer as well as the sermon. Having shared a number of my sermons in several of my books, I thought it might be helpful to share some of my prayers as possible guides for other pastors. I do not encourage ministers to pray the prayers of other preachers but to use them as models for one's own prayer preparation. If the pastor is going to read the prayers, he or she also needs to learn how to pray the prayers, so they sound natural and not rote or monotonous,

I do not claim that I have shared here ideal models of prayers, but they are my modest efforts to offer my prayers for various Sunday worship services. Hopefully, they might serve as a suggested resource for a pastor. Again, I express my appreciation to my friend and fellow minister, Rand Forder, for his careful proof reading of my manuscript.

1.

CALLS TO WORSHIP

A "Call to Worship" summons the worshipper to prepare oneself to worship the Holy God. It should be fairly brief, and both the leader and the members of the congregation share in this summons.

CALL TO WORSHIP

Leader: We open our spirit to God
People: O God, come down.
Leader: We open our spirit to God.
People: O God, come in.
Leader: We open our spirit to God.
People: O God, come among us and make us whole.

CALL TO WORSHIP

Leader: Spirit of God enfold us.
People: Spirit of God cleanse us.
Leader: Spirit of God inspire us.
People: Spirit of God love us.

CALL TO WORSHIP

Leader: We lift sinful hands in worship today.
People: We gather to receive your cleansing grace today.
Leader: We acknowledge our sins and ask for forgiveness.
Unison: Grant us assurance of your love and forgiveness.

CALL TO WORSHIP

Leader: We bring our different gifts to worship God.
People: We affirm our different kinds of services for God.
Leader: We affirm that God's Spirit uses all our gifts and services.
Unison: May we rededicate our gifts and services to God this hour.

CALL TO WORSHIP

Leader: We gather to worship the Living God.
People: We believe that the God of love calls us to worship.
Leader: We believe that God is love and this love is for all persons.
People: May that refreshing love renew our spirits in this hour.

CALL TO WORSHIP

Leader: The Lord be with you!
People: And also, with you.
Leader: Lift up your hearts!
People: We lift our hearts to the Lord.
Unison: We unite our hearts in prayer and praise.

CALL TO WORSHIP

Leader: We raise our voices to proclaim your greatness, O God.
People: We lift our songs of praise to God.
Leader: We extol your love, O God.
People: We worship this loving God of grace and concern for all persons.

CALL TO WORSHIP

Leader: We kneel before the cross of Christ today.
People: May we never forget the cost of this sacrificial love.
Leader: Such love deepens our awareness of our sins.
People: The depth of this love demands our gratitude and allegiance.

CALL TO WORSHIP

Leader: Jesus said, "You are the salt of the earth."
People: Sprinkle us across the world that the flavor of your presence will be apparent
Leader: Jesus said, "You are the light of the world."
People: Let our light shine so all might see you in us.
Unison: May this be so as we gather to worship.

CALL TO WORSHIP

Leader: The God of endless love draws us to this place today.
People: May we be open to the gift of that divine Presence.

Leader: Drawing on this divine love may we strive for justice, peace, and reconciliation with all persons.
People: Help us to live in harmony with all your children, young and old.

CALL TO WORSHIP

Leader: Help us to turn aside in this moment.
People: To set aside our anxious thoughts and concerns.
Leader: To pause and listen, to pay attention and worship.
People: To leave refreshed, enlivened, enlightened, and recommitted.

CALL TO WORSHIP

Leader: Give us a heart to praise God.
People: A heart set free from sin.
Leader: A heart humble, lowly, and contrite.
People: A heart submissive, meek, and redeemed.

CALL TO WORSHIP

Leader: Jesus journeys into our presence this hour.
People: Hosanna, Save us, Jesus.
Leader: Save us from our indifference, our shallow faith, our greed, and jealousy, our weak commitment, and our hard-heartedness.
People: Hosanna. Save us from these and all our sins.

CALL TO WORSHIP

Leader: We confess that too often we are blind and cannot see God's Presence.

People: Open our eyes that we might see through the shadows to discern your nearness.

Leader: Open our mind so that we understand the power of your love and grace.

People: Open our hands that we might offer them in your service.

CALL TO WORSHIP

Leader: We gather to worship our God who knows our name.

People: We confess that we are God's children.

Leader: We know God hears us and cares about our needs.

People: We know God is with us in our trials, difficulties, and suffering.

Unison: We worship God who loves and cares about all our needs and concerns.

CALL TO WORSHIP

Leader: May we open wide the windows of our spirit to God's Spirit.

People: Fill us now with the light of God's grace and love.

Leader: May we open wide the door of our heart.

People: So that as we enter worship, God's Spirit may fill us with a strong sense of the divine Presence and forgiving love.

CALL TO WORSHIP (LABOR DAY WEEKEND)

Leader: We gather this morning to remember God's love and blessings.

People: Forgive us, Lord, when our memory is short, and we fail to remember all your blessings.

Leader: In this time of worship, we reach back into our memory and seek to recall all God has done for us. Help us to affirm boldly:

All: "Bless the Lord O my soul and forget not all his benefits."

CALL TO WORSHIP (COMMUNION)

Leader: Let us prepare our hearts as we gather at the Lord's Table.

People: First, we confess that we have sinned against others, ourselves, and especially God.

Leader: We come to the Lord's Table grateful that God forgives our sins.

Unison: We lift our hearts in gratitude for God's mercy and love.

CALL TO WORSHIP (PALM SUNDAY)

Leader: We lift our palm branches in anticipation of Christ's coming.

People: We raise shouts of praise and adoration to him.

Leader: In a humble and obedient way, Christ reveals his love to us as he journeys toward the cross.

People: Hosanna! Hosanna! We bless his name.

CALL TO WORSHIP (EASTER)

Minister: The tomb is empty, the stone rolled away.

Congregation: Christ is risen, Christ is risen indeed!

Minister: For three days, he lay in that cold and lonely tomb.

Congregation: But God's love cannot be contained -not even by death!

Minister: Thanks be to God, who gives us victory through our Risen Lord.

Congregation: Death has been swallowed up in victory.

Minister: Where, O death, is your victory?"

Congregation: Where, O death, is your sting?

Minister: Christ is risen!

Congregation: He is Risen indeed!

CALL TO WORSHIP (PENTECOST)

Leader: God of Pentecostal fire and wind

People: Pour your spirit upon us this hour.

Leader: Open our mind, heart, and spirit to the transforming power of your Spirit.

People: That we might use our resources in your service.

CALL TO WORSHIP

Leader: Our help is in the name of the Lord, who made heaven and earth.

People: O magnify the Lord with me and let us exalt His name together!

Leader: Let us search and try our ways and turn again to the Lord.

People: I was glad when they said unto me; Let us go into the house of the Lord.

Unison: Let us worship and serve the Lord with gladness!

CALL TO WORSHIP

Leader: The church gathers in the name of Jesus Christ.
People: We come because we have been called to follow him.
Leader: We come to worship God in Jesus' name.
People: We come to sing praises and bow down before him.
Unison: Let us worship in spirit and in truth.

CALL TO WORSHIP

Leader: We gather today to worship God.
People: We pray to be shaped by God's grace and forgiveness.
Leader: We come to open our spirits to God's Spirit.
People: May we be molded to serve by God's love and mercy.

CALL TO WORSHIP

Leader: Hear the Word of God, reflect upon it and prepare to be faithful to it.
People: Blessed is the nation whose God is the Lord (Psalm 33:12).
Leader: Righteousness exalts a nation, but sin is a reproach to any people (Proverbs 14: 34).
People: Jesus said, "He has sent me to proclaim release to the captives and recovering of sight to the blind, to set at liberty those who are oppressed, to proclaim the acceptable year of the Lord" (Luke 4:19).

CALL TO WORSHIP

Leader: Holy, Holy, Holy, Lord God of Hosts.
People: Heaven and earth are full of your glory.
Leader: Glory be to God our Father, our Creator and Redeemer.
People: We lift our voices in praise and adoration as we gather to worship.

CALL TO WORSHIP

Leader: God of Justice and Mercy, we lift our voices to You
People: We confess that we do not always practice justice and mercy.
Leader: Forgive us for our lack of compassion and discernment.
People: Open our hearts and minds to sense the loving way of Christ, our Lord in the way we treat others.

CALL TO WORSHIP

Leader: On our journey of faith, we come seeking God's presence in this hour of worship.
People: Sometimes our pathway seems hard and difficult.
Leader: We seek the assurance that we are not alone in this journey.
Unison: May God's presence be so real to us that we will know that we are never alone in our pilgrimage of faith.

CALL TO WORSHIP

Leader: God of Covenant and Promise, we gather to sense Your Presence this hour.

People: May we hear your assurance that we are your children and a part of your family of grace.

Leader: As your children, we are called to reflect your love and forgiveness.

People: Forgive us when we fall short and guide us to commit ourselves to your Kingdom's work.

Unison: We come seeking to renew our commitment to you this hour.

CALL TO WORSHIP

Leader: We acknowledge that our help comes from God, the Maker of Heaven and earth.

People: We affirm that God is the One who watches over us and will not fail us.

Leader: In the darkness of night, we know that God watches over us and does not slumber or sleep.

People: We gather to worship knowing that God is our sure defense and stronghold.

CALL TO WORSHIP

Leader: In the quietness of this moment, we wait before God.

People: May we listen for God's guidance and support.

Leader: We acknowledge that our life is often filled with temptations, failures, and struggles.

People: As we wait in God's presence, may we be strengthened to meet all the struggles and gratifications that lie ahead of us.

CALL TO WORSHIP

Leader: We gather to worship in this church where many have come for decades.

People: We are grateful for this church and the opportunity to worship.

Leader: Many persons in the past have made possible our worship this Sunday.

People: We lift up our hearts in gratitude and seek to be faithful witnesses for Christ today.

CALL TO WORSHIP

Leader: Come now and lift up your voices in praise to God.

People: We gather to affirm our love and devotion to the Lord.

Leader: We testify that we have experienced God's redeeming love in Jesus Christ.

People: May our assurance of this divine love strengthen us to love others as we have been loved in Christ.

CALL TO WORSHIP

Leader: We gather in this sacred place to express our worship to the Eternal God of the universe.

People: We bring our spiritual gifts to dedicate in the service of Christ.

Leader: We acknowledge that our abilities/gifts are wide-ranging and multi-natured.

People: Knowing how much they are needed, we commit them for service in the Kingdom of God.

CALL TO WORSHIP

Leader: The need for Divine help draws us to this place today.
People: We acknowledge our sins and failures to God today.
Leader: We ask for strength and guidance as we face the struggles and temptations of our daily lives.
People: With the assurance of God's presence in this hour, to offer us direction and strength in all we do, we gather to worship in the name of Jesus Christ.

CALL TO WORSHIP (COMMUNION)

Leader: In the quietness of this sacred place, we gather to worship.
People: Stir our hearts with your divine presence, O God.
Leader: We approach your Sacred Table confessing our sins.
People: May the Bread and Cup remind us of your sacrificial death.

CALL TO WORSHIP

Leader: We gather today to follow Jesus' journey to the cross.
People: Help us to remember his suffering and sacrifice for us.
Leader: May the cross reveal to us the depth and wideness of God's love and grace.
People: Give us the courage to take up our cross and follow Christ in service.

CALL TO WORSHIP

Leader: Eternal God, we gather in this sacred place to worship you.
People: We come seeking to understand why Jesus died on a cross.
Leader: Help us understand the depth of your love that the cross reveals.
People: Thank you for your amazing grace and love.

CALL TO WORSHIP

Leader: We open our hands to receive God's gift of love.
People: We are thankful that God takes our hand in His hand to strengthen and guide us.
Leader: Let us lift our hands in praise to God.
People: Thanks be to God for accepting us and loving us.

CALL TO WORSHIP

Leader: The church gathers to worship in the name of Jesus Christ.
People: We come because we have been called to follow Christ.
Leader: We come to worship God in Jesus' name.
People: We come to sing praises and bow down before Him.
Leader: We strive to love as Christ has loved us.
Unison: Let us worship God in spirit and in truth.

CALL TO WORSHIP

Leader: Eternal God of Love, we pause to praise Your name.
People: Assure us in this hour that You are always near us.

Leader: When we are awake or asleep, assure us of Your divine Presence.

People: May that assurance keep us faithful and strong in all our living.

CALL TO WORSHIP

Leader: God of grace and love, we come to worship You in this hour.

People: Forgive us if we choose to focus too much on ourselves.

Leader: May we seek to put You first in our lives and love You with all our heart.

People: With humble hearts, we want to honor Your name and serve You faithfully.

CALL TO WORSHIP (NEW YEAR)

Leader: We gather to worship to acknowledge that You are our Strength and Guide as we enter this new year.

People: May we open our heart and total being to Your leadership.

Leader: Forgive our sins and self-centeredness.

People: We long to love and serve You with our heart, mind, soul, and strength.

CALL TO WORSHIP

Leader: Eternal God, we know that You love all people regardless of their race or color.

People: Forgive us when we fail to respect and affirm those who are a different color, race, or age than we are.

Leader: As Jesus, Your Son, reached out with love to all and died on the cross that all might have redemption from their sins.

People: May we, who claim Him as Lord, strive to follow his example as we respond to all those who cross our path.

CALL TO WORSHIP (NEW YEAR)

Minister: God is the God of all the ages. Let us praise God's name.

People: From everlasting to everlasting, God is the Lord.

Minister: God has been with us in the past, we will trust God in the year that lies before us.

Unison: We recommit ourselves to God and to worshipping and serving our Lord more faithfully in this New Year.

CALL TO WORSHIP

Leader: Our need for your divine presence draws us to this place today, O God.

People: We acknowledge our sins and our need for forgiveness.

Leader: We thank you, O God, for the sacrificial death of Christ on the cross.

People: May we sense today how the cross of Christ reveals your love and grace

CALL TO WORSHIP

Leader: O give thanks to the Lord and call on His name.

People: It is God who made us, and everything was made by God.

Leader: We enter God's house with thanksgiving and acknowledge our indebtedness to our Creator.

People: For all of God's goodness, we praise God's name and come to worship Him.

2.

INVOCATIONS

An invocation is a brief prayer that calls the worshipper to focus with expectancy on God's Spirit one has come to worship. This is not a pastoral prayer and should seek to equip the worshipper's desire to sense God's presence. I sometimes concluded my invocation with a unison Lord's Prayer with my congregation.

INVOCATION

Lord, we always seem to be in a rush.

Slow us down at this hour so we may not miss the deeper meaning of life.

Forgive us for looking without seeing, hearing without listening, touching without feeling, observing without learning, aging without living. Slow us down now to sense, feel, hear, and know your Presence in this moment. Amen.

INVOCATION

Spirit of God, enfold us.
Spirit of God, cleanse us.
Spirit of God, enliven us.
Spirit of God, love us. Amen.

INVOCATION

God, be in our understanding today.
God, be in our searching today.
God, be in our speaking today.
God, be in our singing today.
God, be in our thinking today.
God, be in our worship today. Amen.

INVOCATION

O God, we come seeking you with all our heart.
O God, we come seeking you with all our soul.
O God, we come seeking you with all our mind.
O God, we come seeking you with all our strength.
Grant that in our seeking, we may find you. Amen.

INVOCATION

Loving God, we acknowledge that we suffer from spiritual malnutrition. So, we come today to be fed by your Spirit. Quench our thirst with the water of your presence. Satisfy our hunger with the bread of your love. May we hunger and thirst no more as your Presence sustains us. Amen.

INVOCATION

O Father, we acknowledge that sometimes our worship is far from what it should be, because You seem so far from us. So, God, here are we, and here are You. May we sense Your presence, and may it be real. May it be so real that our lives shall be different because of it. Amen.

INVOCATION (LENT)

O God, we kneel before the cross today. Help us to remember the costs of such love. Awaken our hearts and spirits to the depth of your sacrificial grace in this hour. In the name of Christ who died for us. Amen.

INVOCATION (LENT)

Love Divine, all other loves excelling, we seek to experience Your love this day as we gather to worship. In this Lenten season, we recall the sacrificial love demonstrated on the cross where Christ died for our redemption. Thank You for such mysterious, universal, profound, and identifying love. May our gratitude be seen in our words, lives, and in all of our living. Through Christ who taught us to pray...

INVOCATION (PALM SUNDAY)

We gather by the roadside again, O Lord, as Jesus comes by. We lift our palm branches to praise his presence. May our shouts of praise not soon turn to words of denial and apathy. Help us to be faithful in our adoration. Amen.

INVOCATION (PALM SUNDAY)

Redeemer Lord, as we gather on this Palm Sunday to celebrate Jesus' entrance into Jerusalem centuries ago, may we open our hearts to allow him entrance into our lives that we might truly praise him as Lord and King of our lives. We celebrate his kingdom and affirm today our desire to be a part of his kingdom today. We pray as our Lord taught us to pray...

INVOCATION (EASTER)

We lift up our voices to shout hallelujah this day for Christ our Lord is risen. We celebrate his triumph over death and the grave. Praise be to you, O God, for the resurrection of Jesus, your Son, and our Savior. May his victorious resurrection give us assurance of life after death as we follow him as our Lord and redeemer. Amen.

INVOCATION (EASTER)

O God of Easter and the resurrected Jesus, we open our spirits to Your living Presence in this hour. May the assurance of the risen Christ guide us in our worship. Tune our hearts and minds to be sensitive to Your Spirit which we know is awaiting us now. In the name of the One who taught us to pray...

INVOCATION (WINTER)

All Caring God, on this cold winter morning, we gather to feel the warmth of Your abiding Presence. May the fiery embers of Your inspiring Spirit cast light on the pathway of the genuine worship of You this hour. Give us confidence that You hear us and love us, through Christ who taught us to pray...

INVOCATION (COMMUNION)

Sustaining God, We gather this morning to commune with You. As we come to the Communion Table, may we sense Your living Presence as the bread of Life. Feed us with Your spiritual Presence so our souls might be truly nourished. We ask in the name of the One who taught us to pray...

INVOCATION (COMMUNION SUNDAY)

O Holy Host, You invite us to commune with You at your Table today. Thank You for including all to sit at Your Holy Table--the weak and strong, rich, and poor, young, and old, those near and those afar, educated, and uneducated, happy, and sad, the gifted and the ordinary. May the Bread that's broken and the cup of sacrificial love refresh and feed our souls this hour. May we leave this Table strengthen anew to serve You more faithfully. Amen.

INVOCATION (ANNIVERSARY SUNDAY)

Eternal God, we gather to worship you on the anniversary Sunday of our church. We thank you for our past and pray for your guidance to worship you today and in the days ahead. We open our heart, mind, and spirit to sense your abiding and redeeming grace. Still our restless souls to connect with you this day, as we pray in the name of the One who taught us to pray...

INVOCATION (ADVENT)

O God of Surprises, who surprised the world by becoming incarnate in a tiny baby laid in a manger. May your abiding presence continue to surprise us by meeting us in our worship this hour. May your presence be surprisingly real. Through Christ who taught us to pray...

INVOCATION (ADVENT)

Come thou long expected Jesus, born to set us free from sin, born to set us free from fear, born to set us free from despair, born to set us free from our failures, born to set us free from sorrow. In this glad season, we gather to celebrate your long-expected birth.

Accept our thankful worship as we come in the name of the one whose birth we celebrate, and who taught us to pray…

INVOCATION (CHRISTMAS)

God of Wonder and Signs, we gather this morning to fulfill the longing in our hearts to celebrate again the joy of your coming among us as a baby in a manger. The wonder of your incarnation is a sign of your love and desire to reveal the depths of your very being. We open our hearts to the mystery of your divine presence in these moments. We affirm anew the divine encounter we experience in the One who taught us to pray…

INVOCATION (NEW YEAR)

God of Alpha and Omega, we acknowledge that you are the beginning and the end. On this first Sunday of the new year and as we begin our journey into this year, we open our spirits to find your Presence to guide us in our worship and in our daily living. We pray this in the name of the One who taught us to pray…

INVOCATION (WINTER)

Redeemer God, on this cold morning, we come aside to sense the warmth of your presence. Nurture our spirits as we seek to draw near to you. May our worship be acceptable to you as we pray in the name of the One who taught us to pray…

INVOCATION (SPRINGTIME)

God of Springtime and all seasons, we open our spirits to be refreshed and renewed by Your Holy Spirit this day. May the sunshine of Your Spirit cast light on the path You would have us follow. As we pray in the name of our Lord who taught us to pray…

Invocation (The Coming Of A New Pastor)

O God of new life, new beginnings, and new birth, bless the new chapter Your people in this holy place will begin next Sunday. May the coming of a new pastor challenge the persons who worship here to be open to the new possibilities You will initiate with them in worship and service. May Your renewed Presence guide them to the possibilities they can be when committed to You. Through Christ who taught us to pray…

General Invocations:

In the quietness of this moment, we open our hearts to your presence, O God. Feed our hunger for your love. Quench our thirst for your grace. Assure us now of that love and grace as we come in the name of the One who taught us to pray…

Bless the Lord, O my soul, and all that is within me bless your holy name. We come now to worship You and sense your presence. Bless us now with the assurance of that presence as we pray as our Lord taught us to pray…

Eternal God, in the quiet and beauty of this sacred place, we gather to sense your presence which can calm and direct our lives. May the grace of your divine presence cast the lengthened shadow that will draw us to You this day. Forgive us for erecting walls of ignorance, fear, and suspicion between us and You. Let the power of your divine love break all barriers down that separate us from your abiding presence today. We come in the name of the One who taught us to pray…

Eternal God, we gather in this sacred place aware that many in our world are engaged in war, suffering and chaos. Guide them to the way of peace and wholeness. Grant us now your inner peace and the assurance of your sustaining presence in this hour. We gather in the name of the One who taught us to pray…

Loving God, we come apart from the noisy world to quiet ourselves in your presence and to be nurtured in your warm embrace. May the breath of your presence in this hour inspire and strengthen us to love and serve You more faithfully. As we follow the One who taught us to pray…

With anticipation and assurance, Eternal God, we gather in this place made holy by past encounters with your Spirit to adore and worship You. Accept our praise as we gather to experience anew your divine love and grace. Through Christ who taught us to pray…

Loving God, on this icy, rainy morning, thaw out our frozen spirits with the warmth of Your Presence. Forgive our cool response to Your eternal love. May the wonder of this love be real to us today as we gather to worship. Through Christ who taught us to pray…

O Creator God, who made possible sunshine and rain, warmth and cold, light, and dark, we gather to praise your name and to offer our worship. We know that our praise never fully extols your greatness, but accept our feeble efforts to express our thanksgiving and adoration as we come to worship in the name of the One who taught us to pray…

O God, we gather to worship this hour with many feelings. When our souls are low in despondency, may the cool breath of your nearness sustain us. May the strong arm of your love undergird us. May the concern of your grace be warmly felt within us, as we lean upon Christ Jesus our Lord for strength in this hour. In his name we pray. Amen.

Loving God, We turn away now from the many distractions of the world around us to focus our attention on worship. So, calm our anxieties, open our hearts, expand our vision, stimulate our awareness, and touch our feelings now with the power of your presence. O God, we want to love you, trust you, follow your way, so awaken our sensitivities to your presence. Through Christ who taught us to pray...

Creator God, we gather today seeking to find a home in Your Presence. Forgive us for not seeing Your Spirit all around us, in the natural world, in the faces of those we meet along our path, in the pain of those who are hurting and in the quietness of this moment. May we sense Your Spirit now in our worship. Through Christ who taught us to pray saying...

O God of eternal life, we pause this day to thank You for the life which begins now through Jesus Christ our Lord. Give us the faith to trust You in this life and in the life to come. Through Jesus Christ, our risen Lord's name, we pray. Amen.

Loving God, we confess that sometimes following You is not easy. It is hard to love you when even our own families and friends do not understand or support us. But teach us, Lord, to be loyal to You and to love You. Give us the courage to bear witness for Christ wherever we are. Give us strength in this hour to love and serve you more faithfully. We pray in the name of Jesus who taught us to pray...

Creator God, as we gather for worship, calm our spirits, open our mind, and heighten our sensitivity to your presence. We know you are present in this place. May we be present to your Presence. Through Christ who taught...

Loving God, we lift our voices in gratitude this day for the gift of life, for the opportunity to worship, for your many blessings, for many occasions to serve you, and proclaim your grace and glory. May we seek to give our lives with an attitude of gratitude as we strive to worship and serve you as we follow in the steps of the One who taught us to pray...

O God, Emmanuel, thank you for the assurance that you are with us in this hour. For those who feel defeated, support them with hope; for the lonely sustain them with your presence; for the grieving reassure them with your comfort; for the guilty, remind them of your forgiveness; for the doubtful, encourage them with confidence; for those feeling unloved, nurture them with your sustaining love, through the One who taught us to pray...

O God of Light and Insight, we gather to worship and acknowledge that too often our eyes have been blind or not opened to your presence. Enable us now to discern your living Presence in our midst through our redeeming Lord who taught us to pray....

Come, Redeemer God into the depths of our hearts this hour. Calm our spirits; nurture our hearts; feed our souls and awaken our senses to the approach of Your divine Spirit. As we come in the name of the One who taught us to pray...

Creator God, We come into Your Presence in worship asking that You create within us a clean heart, a resolute spirit, and a courageous will to serve You more faithfully. May we be open in this hour to Your creative grace in the name of the One who taught us to pray...

Ever Present God, these frigid, snowy days draw us to sense the warmth of Your eternal love. Knowing that love is the essence of Your eternal nature, may we learn to love even as You have loved us. We know You have loved us in creation and through the sacrificial death of Your Son. We acknowledge the love which Christ taught us through his life and words, and affirm that love when we pray as he taught us...

Radiant God, on this bright Sunday morning, we open ourselves to Your Presence. May the brightness of Your Presence guide us; the warmth of Your Presence comfort us; the illuminating power of Your presence inspire us; and the inner glowing radiance of Your Presence assures us that You are with us in these moments of worship. Through Christ who taught us to pray...

Ever Present Father, these frigid, snowy days draw us to sense the warmth of Your eternal love. Knowing that love is the essence of Your eternal nature, may we learn to love even as You have lived us. We know You have love us in creation and through the sacrificial death of Your Son. We acknowledge the love which Christ taught us when we pray...

Loving God, we gather to worship this day sensing your Spirit knocking at our heart's door. May we open and let your Spirit in. Open our eyes to the reality of your Presence. Open our ears to hear your call to respond to your love. Open our minds to discern your directions this day. Open our hands to serve you in all we do. Enter our lives now with the fullness of your grace. Amen.

3.

PASTORAL PRAYERS

A pastoral prayer should not only focus on acknowledging the holiness of the God we are worshipping, but denotes the needs of the congregation that day, expresses an awareness of the problems, concerns, and special happenings in one's city, nation and sometimes the world. It often will affirm our need of God's love, forgiveness, and guidance. It should also reflect something of the theme of the sermon itself but should not be a miniature sermon in itself. One should spend the appropriate time to prepare this prayer and not let it be "something" off the top of one's head.

NEW YEAR

Eternal God, on this first Sunday of' the New Year, we pause to ask for a sense of direction from Your hand in our own personal living, in our life as a congregation, in our nation, and in the world. We pray, O Lord, that Your Spirit will work within the hearts of all persons to bring about peace.

Now we commit this present time to worship you. We come to fortify ourselves and to be strengthened to serve you more effectively. We give to you all of the anxieties we have about the future and our uncertainties about the roads of life ahead of us. Our faith has been built on the confidence and assurance of your presence with us in the past. We turn now and look toward the future. As a child trusts its parents, as the birds trust the air, the animals their instincts, so we lean in trust upon you and your grace. Give us the assurance that your strong arm will bear us up no matter what our difficulty is. We trust you whether our burden is grief or a family member who is ill or a family member who is across the seas, or we are crushed by a load of depression. May we have a strong sense of your presence to lift us up.

On this first Sunday of the New Year, we open our spirits to your Spirit so we might be led by your hand, feel the strength of your grace and love, and the breath of your presence within us. Lord, we wait now in confidence for your guidance in all that we think and do. We pray this in the name of Jesus Christ, our living Lord. Amen.

MARTIN LUTHER KING, JR DAY

O Loving God of all persons, we gather in this sacred place, which has been made holy by your presence and with the gathering of faithful Baptists for almost two centuries, to worship and adore your name. Thank you for loving us in spite of our weaknesses and prejudices. We turn to the power of your all-inclusive love to cleanse us and make us more accepting and loving of all persons regardless of their race or sex. Forgive us when we have been blinded by our prejudices, indifferences, affluence, isolation, greed, or hardness of heart in our relationship with others around us. Help us to be more Christ-like as we live and minister in your world.

We pray today for Barack Obama who will be inaugurated as our 44th President on Tuesday. We express our gratitude that an African American can now rise to such a high office in our country. May his term in this high office help lead our country beyond our racial prejudices and discrimination. We know what a difficult assignment awaits him with our nation's economy in peril, our enormous debt, our involvement in several wars on the other side of the world, the failure or struggles of many financial, business and automobile institutions, the crisis in our health care and educational areas, and many other challenging issues. We pray for him wisdom, guidance, insight, moral character, courage, perseverance, confidence, religious depth, fairness, a gracious and generous spirit, endurance, faithfulness and an abiding confidence in your guidance and presence. Whether we voted for our new President or not, give us, Lord, the sense of presence to support and pray for him as the President now of all our nation's peoples, regardless of the color of our skin. Bless our new President and our nation and guide us to let liberty prevail for all our people and let justice roll down, and righteousness be exalted in our land as we defend and live out the words of our nation's Constitution.

Now in the quietness of this moment we open our spirits to your divine Spirit. Bless us with the warming embrace of that Spirit as we gather here. Through Christ who reached out to all persons with his inclusive love and grace, we pray. Amen.

LENT

Eternal God, sometimes we confess that we, too, feel forsaken like our Lord. We feel forsaken, abandoned, isolated, and alone. There are times when we want to scream: "God, where are You?" You seem so far removed from us, so silent to our needs, so unconcerned, so remote, so distant. Our agonies and burdens press down upon us, and You do not seem available or concerned. You are so far removed from us that we want to cry rivers of tears. Sometimes we simply want to whisper. We long to whisper our concerns, hopes, and dreams to know that You hear and that You care. Assure us now, we pray.

O God, we do not want this distance to be between us. Is it of our own making? Is it something that we have done? Show us Your nearness, Your available presence. Forgive us, O God, for the sin which always separates us from You.

May we learn from our own Lord's suffering and agony that You are always present and near to us, seeking to meet our needs even when we do not know it. We open ourselves now like fertile soil to let Your spirit rain the love of Your grace upon us. Bathe us in the sunshine of Your radiant love. May our spirits grow warm as they are embraced by Your presence this hour. Through Jesus Christ our living Lord, we pray. Amen.

LENT

Eternal God, it is difficult for us to understand the amazing love of Jesus for others in his agony and sorrow. Thank you for such love. Teach us how to accept your gracious forgiveness and then in turn to extend the same forgiving spirit to others. May we follow the Christ, who through word and deed forgave all.

O God, like the penitent thief on the cross, we come to you with our struggles and uncertainties, yet we come trusting. Give us a renewed faith and the courage to face life with the knowledge that we can lean upon you, and that you will not let us down. We trust you, Lord, with that which we have seen, heard, and experienced in Jesus Christ. Eternal Father, we thank you for your love and the depth of the love we have seen at the cross of Christ. We thank you for the compassion we saw revealed. O God, we express our inadequacy at trying to understand our Lord's sense of abandonment. We tremble at the edge of this mystery. But, O God, whatever it means, we know that it assures us now that we are no longer separated from you. Our sins have been laid on him. Because of what Christ has done for us, we can have communion with you. Thank you, God, for such costly love. Through Jesus Christ, who gave his all, we pray. Amen.

LENT

Eternal Father, you have loved us with an everlasting love, and we focus this day upon that living Word which was made flesh in Jesus Christ. We pause to stand again before that cross today.

We stand amazed at the length, height, breadth, depth of such love, a love that suffered, cared, and died for us. We stand before this cross burdened to think that our world could slay its best and its highest.

Yet we also know that we stand before that cross as those who continually reject the highest. We confess how often we choose the lower instead of the higher; the weaker instead of the stronger; the perverse instead of the righteous; mediocrity instead of our best; and apathy instead of involvement. Give us the courage to sense your forgiving grace.

Forgive us that we are more willing to be instructed or reformed than we are to be redeemed. Open each of us to an ever new and deeper understanding of our Savior's death. Grant that we may never be casual as we stand before the event which has taxed the skills of the finest poets, musicians, scholars, and preachers. Keep us reachable and pliable, open, and responsive to your grace. May we be willing captives to the wonder of it all.

Stir us now to such new intentions that we will seek to die to self and live to Christ. May we stand as new people before that love which is so amazing and so divine. May we be embraced by that love and go forth to live and serve in the name of the Christ, who gave his all for us, we pray. Amen.

PALM SUNDAY

Eternal God, we come this day to praise You as we reflect upon the entrance of Christ to Jerusalem and as we look upon the cross of Christ. We have sensed Your grace through the world around us, in the hush of snowfall in the winter, in the power of a driving rain, in the splendor of a starlit night, in the warmth of the sun on a cold day, in the beauty of spring and in the continuous cycle of the seasons.

Nevertheless, O God, we confess that there are times when Your voice seems so silent to us. In the face of pain, suffering, rejection, tragedy, defeat, evil, war and death, we long to hear Your words of support and encouragement. Sometimes Your Spirit seems far from us. We do not feel the warmth of Your presence, but instead we often feel that Your back is turned away from us. Show us through the suffering of Your Son on the cross the depth of Your concern, Your love, and Your abiding Presence.

We await Your Presence now in this hour. We open our hearts to sense Your coming. Surprise us with Your Presence. May we be assured of Your love, sustained by Your power, and strengthened by Your grace. Touch us now by Your loving Presence as we pray it in the name of Jesus Christ, our living Lord. Amen.

EASTER

Eternal God, who raised Jesus Christ from the dead, we praise Your grace and love. The wonder of the living presence of Christ thrills our hearts. Thank You for the assurance we have of life and eternal life through His resurrection. We rejoice in Your inclusive grace which reaches out to persons regardless of race or sex. Like Mary Magdalene, John, Paul, and others who were witnesses to the risen Lord, open our eyes and ears to sense, feel, see, and hear Christ's living presence with us today. May the new life we experience in Christ affect everything we do and say.

Almighty God, the Alpha, and the Omega, the One who is, and who was, and who is to come, we praise You for Your redeeming grace. Strengthen us by Your living presence to rise from doubt to faith, skepticism to conviction, defeat to victory, and fear to peace. Gird us, O Living One, with the strength of Your strong right hand to face the difficulties of life and the terrors of death with the assurance of Jesus Christ, Your faithful witness. Amen.

EASTER

O Creator, Ever Creating, Living God, we gather in this sacred space on Easter Sunday to sense Your divine, eternal presence to affirm in our uncertain and bewildering mind the meaning and reality of the resurrection of Jesus Christ. We know it is central to our faith and we long to have a clearer assurance of its possibility. Like the disciple Thomas, we long to touch and see the nail prints in the hands and feet of Jesus and the wound in his side that we might know for sure that it is really he. We confess that we are such sensory people. How can we really believe if we can't see for ourselves? Yet those first disciples struggled with this same question, Thomas most of all. And you came to them, and they did indeed see and believe. And Thomas finally did believe even without touching.

Is there some way we can possibly see and be assured today 2000 years later? That's all we want, Lord. Is it really too much to ask for? Critics abound everywhere, Lord. They say that a dead person cannot come back again, and all this resurrection talk is nonsense. If that is really true, why, and how did the Church come into existence? Why would the first disciples have been willing to die as martyrs for a lie or an illusion? They believed they really saw You, Lord. You were not a fantasy or mirage to them but the same yet different living person they had known before the crucifixion. Your Presence convinced, persuaded, assured, swayed, energized, and revitalized them. So, come now again on this Easter Sunday and breathe that breath of reassurance into our too often unbelieving spirits with the confidence of the early disciples and the Apostle Paul that we might proclaim boldly that Christ is risen and that he is risen indeed! We ask in Jesus' name. Amen.

MOTHER'S DAY

Eternal Creator, we come to You this day thanking You for the wonder, mystery, and beauty of the home. We thank You for what our home has meant, for the nurture of good parents and for the faithfulness of children who have responded to life and committed themselves to causes with meaning and purpose. Give us a willingness to listen openly to our parents and children, even when they have failed. Forgive us for wallowing in self-pity or condemning or blaming instead of being willing to lift others up and understand them.

We thank You for the joys we have shared together within our home. Teach us how to celebrate these times more fully. We also thank You for Your presence with us in the sorrows that we have experienced. Teach us how to embrace each other more fully and lift each other up in times of difficulties and when burdens are heavy.

For those in our fellowship this day who are single, having never been married, divorced, or widowed, we pray that they will sense Your companionship in the home that they have within this Christian community and note our love and devotion. Teach us how to love one another, how to be good parents, if we have children, and also how to be faithful in our relationship with each other and dedicated in our commitment to You. Teach us, O Lord, to seek to love even as we have been loved through Jesus Christ. For we pray in His strong name. Amen.

COMMENCEMENT SUNDAY

Eternal God, we come today aware that we have not made ourselves and we really cannot keep ourselves nor forgive ourselves, so we reach out to You. We thank You for Your creation, our preservation, and redemption. We thank You for the wonderful challenge of living and for the opportunity of becoming Your children. Teach us how to grow and to be nurtured in our faith.

We thank You for our seniors today who are graduating from high school. Bless them as they close one chapter in their lives and begin a new one. Strengthen their faith as they face the exciting new challenges which lie before them. Give them the courage to stand for Christian values and to grow in their knowledge of You. May they feel Your presence when the going gets tough and they feel lonely, confused, or tempted. As the years pass, may they remember what they have been taught in this sacred place.

We thank You for this church and for its commitment to service, teaching, love, and as Your witness in this community. We come this day also acknowledging those in our fellowship who have grief, who have experienced illness, have known accidents, hardships, or pain. We ask You to sustain them.

Open our eyes as we come to this place that we might sense Your strong presence. Open our ears so that we might hear the sounds of Your presence. Open our hearts that we might feel Your presence. Open our minds that we might think Your thoughts after You. We come today searching to love You with our total being. Through Jesus Christ our Lord, we pray. Amen.

SEEKING LOVE

Eternal God, we come to worship today to be loved and to love. May we hear Your voice calling us today to be, to serve and to give. We have been taught that Your spirit is love. We pray that You will teach us how to know the meaning of love, especially Your love. May we learn to listen to its many voices. May we hear the sound of love in the greeting of a friend, the sighing sleep of a baby, the exchanging of vows at the marriage altar, the laughter of children at play, in words of encouragement in times of need, and in the forgiving words of Your acceptance of us.

Forgive us for putting our faith in force and might instead of love. Forgive us for putting our faith in wealth and prestige instead of love. As men and women in the past saw Your love in Jesus Christ, so now may we let them see the love of Jesus Christ in us today. May they see it in the hand we extend to lift up someone who has fallen, as we listen to a friend pour out his or her difficulties. May love be seen in our concern for the needy, the lonely, the bereaved, the hurting, and suffering of those around us.

We lift our voices humbly as we thank You for Your blessing, and we praise Your name. Thank You for all You continue to do for us daily. When we feel discouraged, give us hope; in our sorrowing, give us comfort; in our unbelieving, give us faith; in our suffering, give us assurance; when we are lonely, give us companionship; when we feel hopeless, give us courage.

O God, who loves all the world, love each of us today. We confess that there are times that we feel so unlovable because of our sins. We feel unclean, filthy, misguided, perplexed, and saddened. Love us still. May the embrace of Your presence be so real that we will know the assurance of Your forgiving love. Touch us, forgive us, redeem us, direct us. O love that will not let us go; we rest our weary souls in You. We give You back the life we owe, that we may richer, fuller be. In the loving name of Jesus Christ our Lord, we pray. Amen.

MEMORIAL DAY

Eternal God, loving Shepherd of our souls, we pause now to thank You again for the gift of life, for the gift of rain and sunlight, for their beauty and the assurance from their moisture and light that life continues. As we approach a new season, may we use this time to re-evaluate our own purpose for living. Help us to sense our own dependence upon Your gracious hand. We know that we cannot control what happens within the natural world. But we can seek to control what happens within our own lives as we recommit them to You. Help us to use this hour to think, to pray and to recommit ourselves to seeking You that we might grow spiritually. Help us so that we might lean upon the power of Your strong presence in this hour.

We pause to thank You today for those who died for our country. We acknowledge that their sacrifices have helped us maintain our country, freedom, and values. Help us not to forget their love and devotion. May we seek to make our country always safe and secure.

We pray now that You will bless this day those who are hurting. May they sense Your healing love. Bless those on this day who are mourning. May they sense Your healing love. Bless those who are ill. May they sense Your healing love. Bless those who feel guilty. May they sense Your healing love. Bless those who are aware of their sins. May they sense Your forgiving grace. Bless those who think too highly of themselves. Heal them. Bless those who think too lowly of themselves. Heal them with Your grace.

Bless us now as we come to this place of worship. May Your love and grace be so real to us that we will leave here different people because of having met You in this place. Through Jesus Christ, our Lord, we pray. Amen.

FATHER'S DAY

Our Father, Eternal Parent, we pause today to sense the embrace of Your loving presence. We know You are here. May we be present to Your presence. We long to love and serve You better. Help us to model our lives after Your Son, Jesus, who has taught and lived the way You would have us live.

We confess our sins and weakness. Forgive us. May the inspiration of Your Presence in this hour strengthen us to withstand the shadows or voices that would lead us down wrong paths or into forbidden territory. May we lean upon Your strong arm for guidance and protection.

We remember the many people across our land and world who are the victims of prejudice because of the color of their skin or their status or their income. May the abiding presence of Your grace sustain them. Help us to work and worship together as brothers and sisters in Christ. Help us to love others as You have loved us unconditionally. May law and justice prevail throughout our land. Give us the courage to join hands with all those who love and serve You.

We pray especially today for all the fathers in our congregation. Help us to strive to be the best father we can be. May we always make our family the highest priority. We acknowledge that we have not always done our best but we genuinely long to reach for our ideals.

We come now to learn how to be better Christians. May we sense Your strong love and direction. Through Christ, our Lord, we pray. Amen.

COMMUNION SUNDAY

Eternal God, in just a few moments we shall come to commune with you at Your table. We come to this table aware that it is Your table and not ours. We come to acknowledge that we have no right or place of our own at this table. None of us deserves to sit at Your right hand. We come at your invitation.

So, we come to confess our sins and acknowledge that we are all sinners saved by grace. We have all betrayed Your love. We have envied, lusted, coveted, stolen, denied, broken our promises, yet you have given Your body to be broken for us. You have had your veins broken and emptied of blood for us. What a feast of love you have given us. What priceless redemption you have bestowed upon us! Forgive us once more, O God, and receive us as repentant followers who cannot live without this table.

Thank you for your forgiving grace. let the blood from your wounded side overflow, cleanse, and make us white as snow. Lift us from our brokenness and despondency as you lifted your first disciples and make us once again into a church of power in your kingdom. Baptize us in your Holy Spirit so that all things may become new. May this table truly sit at the center of our lives. For yours is the kingdom, the power, and the glory forever. Amen.

COMMUNION

O God of every time and place, we thank You for the assurance that You are with us at this particular time and in this particular place. Some of us come to worship this morning with our lives filled with great joy and enthusiasm for living. We are excited about our jobs or retirement; our family life is good, and our whole life seems to swell with a sense of radiance.

Others come this morning for whom life is difficult. Their burdens are heavy. They have experienced loneliness, depression, anxiety, fear, or some physical problem. So, this morning we pray that Your spirit will nourish them and sustain them with Your grace, We pray that whatever our needs are this day that we shall bring them to You with the assurance that You hear us and that You sustain us.

As we come to Your Table this morning, we pray that You will give us the assurance of Your living presence that can minister to us whatever our needs are. Cleanse us from our sins; forgive us for our wrongdoing and guide us into the tomorrows.

We thank You for Christ who by his life, teachings, and death demonstrated to us the power of service and sacrifice. Enable us to follow his example and to seek to live and serve You in the world. Through Jesus Christ our Lord, we pray. Amen.

COMMUNION

Eternal Father, we come reaching out this morning. We come reaching .out to know you; to understand your way and to follow your will and obey your command. We come reaching out for you, but sometimes you seem hidden from us and distant. Help us to sense your reaching out toward us with your concern and your nearness. We come this morning seeking to reach out to know other people. We confess that there are barriers that separate us from others through misunderstandings, hurts, wrongs, and sins, and we ask forgiveness. Teach us how to apologize, how to love, understand, and care. O Lord, teach us this day how to reach out to know and love others better.

Help us also, O Lord, to know how to reach out to ourselves. We confess that too often we feel pulled in all directions by family, jobs, and friends. We feel as though we could sometimes fly all to pieces. So, we pray today that you will pull us together and make us whole. Give us that sense of redemption, wholeness, healing that comes from your Spirit. We come this day, O Father, reaching out to know you, others, and ourselves better. Touch us with your presence as we commune at your Table. We come to this Table to remember your Son's death and sacrifice for us. The extent of your love has been supremely seen in the death of Jesus Christ, your Son, and our Lord. In his strong name we pray. Amen.

COMMUNION

O Breath of God, breathe upon us the awareness of your abiding presence as we come into this sacred space set apart to worship You. May we sense Your nearness and love. We gather at Your Table to be fed by Your Presence. As we eat the bread and drink the cup, be in our tasting and reflecting, swallowing, and remembering, speaking, and hearing, sensing, and responding. Inspire us with Your Presence to a more gracious living. Inspire us to love and serve You more faithfully. Thank You for loving us even when we make journeys into the far country and waste our inheritance in foolish ways.

Open our eyes to see that You are with us

on bright days and on dark ones…
in the good and in the bad.…
in health and in sickness.…
in our failures and in our victories.…
in our joys and in our pain.…
in our laughter and in our tears.…
in the bread and in the cup.…
in our heart and at the Table.…
in our living and in our dying.…

Give us eyes to see Your presence everywhere and ears to hear the movement of Your presence all around us and within us. Amen.

COMMUNION SUNDAY

COMMUNION

O loving God, we gather this day to worship You. Our presence here in this place affirms our dependence upon You. Our journey through life is often difficult and hard unless we are fed by Your spirit, so we come to Your Table to experience the power of Your Presence pulsating through our veins. As we drink this cup, may we feel the strength of Your grace sustaining us so that we will thirst no more. As we eat this bread, may we be fed by the Bread of Heaven. Nourish us until our will, desire, hope, and dreams become Your will and goals as we eat at Your Table. We offer You our mind, heart, soul, and strength. O Bread of Life, feed us until we are fully nourished to live for You.

We bring before You our burdens, sorrows, illnesses, hurts, needs, and pains and pray for the assurance of Your abiding presence. Thank You, Lord, that nothing separates us from Your love. In times of difficulty this knowledge comforts us. We come to Your Table with our joys and happiness to express our thanksgiving for the wonder of living. O Bread of Heaven, we come to Your Table that we may hunger and thirst no more. Feed us with Your abundant grace. Through Christ, whose death revealed Your sacrificial love to us. Amen.

COMMUNION

Eternal God, You have blessed us with food to nourish our bodies, and we thank You for our physical food. We come now to nourish our souls with spiritual food. Feed us as the Bread of Life. You have blessed us with water to quench our thirst on a hot day. We come now to drink from Your fountain of living water. Feed us until we hunger and thirst no more.

We· know, Lord, that there are persons in our congregation who are hurting today. They have known the pains of illness and grief, moving into a new community, new beginnings, loneliness, anxiety, separation, fear, or some kind of tragedy. We thank You for the assurance that nothing separates us from Your love. We long to sense the embrace of Your supportive grace today. O Shepherd of our souls, we need Your tender care. We pray to be more sensitive to Your presence.

Come now, O God, in the midst of our routine worship, tired spirits, and unexpected attitudes, and worn habits and surprise us with the moving power of Your spirit. Open our minds, warm our hearts, enlighten our thinking, encourage our spirits, and empower our efforts to serve You more effectively. Through Christ, who loves us and goes before us and guides us and directs us into the challenging days which lie before us. Amen.

COMMUNION

Eternal God, we acknowledge that you are holy, and we are ordinary. You are Spirit and we are mortal. You are eternal and we are transient. Yet You call us to worship You in this place and at this time. We ask You to accept our confession of our sins and grant us Your forgiveness. We gather at this sacred Table to worship You. We long to love You, understand Your way better and to know You. Hence, we gather before Your Table today.

We bring our sins, pain, burdens, doubts, fears, grief, and brokenness to You. Heal us with Your love. Forgive us with Your grace. May the radiance of Your grace and love give us peace and joy.

We come to Your Table to commune with You. Speak to us through the Bread and Cup, the words and silence, the mystery and simplicity of this moment. May Your presence be real to us in this hour, O God. We come to Your Table to sense Your nearness and your abiding grace. Amen.

COMMUNION

O loving God, we gather this day to worship You. Our presence here in this place affirms our dependence upon You. Our journey through life is often difficult and hard unless we are fed by Your spirit, so we come to Your Table to experience the power of Your Presence pulsating through our veins. As we drink this cup, may we feel the strength of Your grace sustaining us so that we will thirst no more. As we eat this bread, may we be fed by the Bread of Heaven. Nourish us until our will, desire, hope, and dreams become Your will and goals as we eat at Your Table. We offer You our mind, heart, soul, and strength. O Bread of Life, feed us until we are fully nourished to live for You.

We bring before You our burdens, sorrows, illnesses, hurts, needs, and pains and pray for the assurance of Your abiding presence. Thank You, Lord, that nothing separates us from Your love. In times of difficulty this knowledge comforts us. We come to Your Table with our joys and happiness to express our thanksgiving for the wonder of living. O Bread of Heaven, we come to Your Table that we may hunger and thirst no more.

Feed us with Your abundant grace. Through Christ, whose death revealed Your sacrificial love to us. Amen.

LABOR DAY

Eternal God, We acknowledge today that you are the eternal worker, the one who has created life, sustains it, directs it, and upholds it. Enable us to sense what your work is like so that we ourselves might learn to participate in your creative and ongoing labor.

We thank you for the work we have. We thank you for work which we can do with our minds so we can solve problems, think, plan, and study. We thank you for the work that we can do with our backs, for the strength and power we have to dig, construct, and build. We thank you for the work we can do with our hands where we can draw, write, and guide, direct, and move machinery and equipment. We thank you for feet that can carry us in different directions as we stand, walk, or run in service for you. Teach us to learn to work with all of our senses and bodily functions to serve you in a more meaningful way.

We pray today for those who are seeking to find purpose and meaning within their work. May our work give us joy, and may it become an avenue for service for you. Help those who labor in the midst of the monotonous to find a higher meaning and a deeper goal. We thank you for young people who are preparing themselves to serve and labor in the future. Give them a sense of vision and purpose, discipline, and direction. Give us guidance as we seek to lead them.

We thank you also for leisure in life, for the opportunity to pause so that we might sense your presence as it breathes the fresh breath of your spirit upon us. We come worshiping now in the name of Jesus Christ our living Lord. Amen.

INDEPENDENCE DAY

Eternal God, we thank You for allowing us to live in such a challenging time as this. We pause today to pray for the citizens and leaders of our nation. Help us so that we shall always seek to place your standards of integrity, morality, justice, and righteousness above the loyalty to any party or government. Forgive us when we identify nationalism with Christianity and interpret any political way of life as blind allegiance to You. May we always seek to work that Your kingdom shall come and that Your will may be done on earth as it is in heaven.

Make us aware of our own problems and difficulties within our nation. We confess that sometimes we almost feel overwhelmed by inflation, our national debt, famine, poverty, and all of the problems in the world. Lord, make us worthy of these challenges. May we seek to be a part of the force in the world to set the wrong right and to lift the fallen, to guide those who are misdirected and to correct the distortions within us and within society. Help us to comfort the bereaved and overcome evil with good. We are aware that our part will not be an easy one, but with Your strength and guidance, we can help overcome the problems in our land and around the world. In this challenging day, give us confidence which is born of a faith in Your presence that we may know who we are and whose we are and why we are.

Out of Your infinite love, O God, minister to us now in our own special needs. Give us mastery of our own work and sins. Give us the ability to smile even on the worst of days. And give us the courage to persevere when the end and the good seem to elude our grasp. Give us the courage to resume life alone, when parted from those we love. Give us the grace to acknowledge our guilt and sin and the humility to accept Your forgiveness and grace. All of this we ask in the name and to the glory of Jesus Christ, our living Lord. Amen.

In A Storm

Eternal God, as the thunder roars around us and the rains beat upon the earth, may the noise and turmoil within our own souls sense the calm and peace of your spirit. As each of us faces the greatest fear of all, the fear of death, may we confront this fear with the confidence we have received from our Lord Christ. May we commit our soul into your hands and trust you even as our Lord Jesus Christ did. We pray it in his name. Amen.

Stewardship Sunday

Eternal God, some of us will be uncomfortable in Church today. We will wiggle in our seats and let our minds wander because we really do not want to think about our faith and our pocketbook. Some of us are caught unaware that that is what we will deal with today. Forgive us for wanting so much for your Kingdom to come and your will to be done and yet not being willing to support your cause with our lives and possessions. Forgive us for giving so little and expecting so much. Forgive us for giving so little and wondering why the church struggles so much for its survival and often makes such a small dent in the sins of humanity. Give to us this day a sense of vision of the sacrifices that others have made in the past that we might enjoy the freedom to worship here and now.

Lord, when we have received so much and are surrounded by the sacrifices others have made, why then are we still so willing to give so little? Give us a vision of what your Church can become when each of us is dedicated to your work. We are thankful for the salvation that we have experienced through Jesus Christ our Lord.

Grant, O God, that our very lives shall reflect a new dedication to you. May our money, time, and total life become instruments to bear your love and grace to all persons. May we learn to hear and to live by the words of Christ that "it is more blessed to give than to receive." May we learn to mean these words through him who died that we might live. Help us to be givers of love and blessings to others. We who have accepted your great gift, the gift of your son Jesus Christ, and the gift of our own lives, grant that we shall learn to give cheerfully. As we give in the name of Jesus Christ, our living Lord. Amen.

THANKSGIVING

Eternal God, we come to You in prayer this day with a sense of thanksgiving for all the gifts that we have received from Your hand. We thank You for the gift of life, love, work, play, hopes, dreams, and tasks to be done. We thank You for the sacrifices and ideals we have inherited from our forefathers and foremothers who pioneered the way that we might live and exist in this particular time in our history as a nation.

Today we confess that too often we come to You only with our problems. So, on this day we pause to say thank You. We thank You for accepting us when we are really unacceptable. We thank You for hope when we have lost our dreams, for Your presence when we feel abandoned. Thank You for all the wonder, mystery, and beauty in our world; for the touch of friends when the burdens of life get heavy; for moments of silence in a busy world. We thank You for Your hand of assurance when life crashes in upon us, for the joy of helping others when they are in need; for the assurance that You have made a place for each of us when we feel inadequate. We thank You for the gift of life when we feel defeated, for the struggles of life when we become too complacent. We thank You for Your peace in times of fear, for forgiveness when we fail and sin, and for Your love when we feel unloved.

But above all, Father, we are grateful for the sense of Your sustaining power that has come through Your grace that continually blesses us. Give us now in this service a sense of thanksgiving that is so real that all that is within us will constantly praise Your name. Through Jesus Christ who loves us and gave himself for us, we pray. Amen.

ADVENT

O gracious God, as we come into this advent season, once again our minds return to the celebration of the coming of Your Son into the world. Help each of us to begin making preparation for that day as we seek to make room anew for the Christ within our hearts. As we prepare for the Christmas celebration within our homes, may we pause and look inwardly to focus on the deep meaning of the birth of Your Son.

We thank You for this season and its beauty. May we learn to use this time to pause and think about Your great love. As we reflect on Your greatness and holiness, may we be reminded of our own sinfulness and our need to confess our sins and seek to find release from them. Give us forgiveness and peace within from a sense of Your loving grace.

In this Christmas season, may the wonder of Christmas excite us once more. May we become as children and open ourselves to its wonder and beauty to receive the gift that You have given to us through Jesus Christ Your Son. May our own giving reflect the fact that we have sensed and received the great gift of Your love.

May our celebration of Christmas be deeper and more meaningful because we have been drawn closer to You as we reflect on the great gift of Your Son. We pray in this season that we might know Your love anew and love You more deeply. Through Jesus Christ our Lord, we pray. Amen.

ADVENT

Eternal God, as we come into this Christmas season, may we make room again within our hearts for Your Son to find lodging.

Open our eyes that we might see Your coming in the ordinary, unexpected places around us. Help us to open our ears so that we might be able to hear again the singing of angels. May we hear the glad good news that they brought centuries ago, and may we hear it again today. Open our hearts and mouths that we might proclaim the gospel to all persons so that they too might hear the good news. Open our minds that we might have the insight of those wise men who came searching for the Christ child as they followed a distant star. Open our spirits so that we might sense Your Presence in the midst of all our rushing and busyness.

Open divine light to us in our dark moments; encouragement in our times of fear; hope in our despair; peace in our turmoil. Open us to experience joy even in our sorrows and strength in the midst of our weaknesses. Open us to experience wisdom in our times of confusion and a sense of the forgiveness of our sins. Open us again in this Christmas season to experience the tenderness of Your Spirit. May our hearts, minds and total beings be open to sense Your coming as we have never known it before. Through Jesus Christ our Lord whose birth we celebrate in this Christmas season. Amen.

ADVENT

Eternal Father, some of us confess today that we are not yet in the mood for Christmas. We say that we can't catch the spirit. We focus on the wrong places and wrong things. The weather is not right. We can't think what gift we ought to get and there are so many preparations yet to be done. Break through our unpreparedness and whisper the meaning of Christmas to us.

Whisper through the stars as they remind us of the star that men followed to the Christ-child centuries ago. Whisper through the needs of infants and children around us that we might not ignore them but love them. Whisper to us through the warmth and companionship of our own families as we remember the family of Jesus. Whisper to us about Christmas through our work and study as we dedicate it to you. Whisper to us through the merriment of the season.

Whisper to us the joy of Christ about whom the angels sang. Whisper to us through our gift-giving that we might remember that we have received the world's most precious gift as we have sensed it in the birth of your son, Jesus Christ. In this Christmas season, whisper to us, O God, so that Your Spirit shall warmed our hearts and draw us closer to you as we sense your coming anew within this Christmas season, for we pray it in the name of Jesus Christ our living Lord. Amen.

ADVENT

O God, Eternal Father, how glad we are to be alive at Christmastime. We are glad to see the sunlight and the starlight. We are glad for loved ones who are near, glad for the laughter ringing through our rooms and homes, glad greetings in the halls of church and at work. We are glad for Christmas carols; glad for Christmas messages found in the mail; and glad for the wonder and excitement of little children; glad for countless deeds of kindness and love. We are glad above all else for memories for the old and ever new story of Your corning among us in a baby's small form.

We are glad for the One who is the everlasting truth and unspeakable beauty and the Incarnate goodness which has been wrapped in swaddling clothes and was found lying in a manger. Gladden others around us, O Father, through the contagious joy that Christ has given to us May the miracle of Christ and Christmas spread around the world as we pray it in the name of the One whose birth we celebrate this day, even Jesus Christ our living Lord. Amen.

ADVENT

Eternal Giving God, Forgive us as we have often bestowed gifts on all others at Christmas time, but have forgotten the One for whose birthday we have come to celebrate. Show us the way to put Christ on our Christmas list. May we know that his cause needs our time and our energy and our money.

Make us now more alert than ever to those human needs with which Christ identified himself. Help us to see the needs of those who are ill fed or poorly clothed, sad, rejected, and outcast. Though we act foolishly in other ways, our Father, grant us the genius for giving the needed gift at this appropriate time where it will do the most good to those who are in no way able to repay us. May this gift of ourselves enable us to celebrate Christmas all year long in the spirit of the One who was Your gift to humankind.

Gracious God, never let us become discouraged when we realize that Your spirit seemed to have such a small beginning in the world, yet its impact is beyond measuring. In this season we celebrate that we have seen your Spirit as it has come in the form of a baby at Bethlehem. Save us from a sense of despondency when we are tempted to be dejected by the terrible power of evil in the world.

In a world filled too much with terrorism and war, help us to learn to follow the lead of the angels as they announced on the night of our Savior's birth "Peace on earth, good will toward all people." Help us to wage peace as we follow the "Prince of Peace," born in this sacred season. Teach us the way of peace in the world, and may it begin in each of us in this Christmas season.

May we sense from the birth of Christ at this time of celebration, that it is his birthday that we commemorate and not Caesar or Herod's. May we then take hope, and trust that You will enable us to sense by the power of Your Spirit that You are still at work in the world, in ways that are somehow only faintly seen.

Increase our faith that we shall know that in the end Your will shall prevail. May all our days in this Christmas season become for us a time in which we shall be drenched in the powerful Spirit of Your love, peace, and grace, as we come praying in the name of Jesus Christ, our living Lord.

CHRISTMAS EVE

Revealing God, on this Christmas Eve, we pause to express to You thanksgiving for Your great love toward us. As we continue in our preparation to celebrate the birth of Christ, may we focus on Your love that we have experienced supremely in Jesus Christ. In all of our busyness, preparations, and gift buying, may we remember the One who was the greatest gift of all to us, Your Son Jesus Christ, our Lord, for whom this day is celebrated.

Enable us as we reflect on our Lord's birth to remember his care and concern for others as well. May we reflect our love toward You by showing concern for the poor, the hungry, and the needy. We express thanksgiving for some signs of peace around the world. We pray that the One who is the Prince of Peace will continue to work in areas where turmoil continues. We pray that You will be with the people in Bosnia and all of those in other places today who are in the midst of unrest. May the One who is the Prince of Peace slowly bring peace to the parts of the world where clashes continue.

On this Christmas Eve help us to remember the greatness of Your gift to us. Knowing that Your incarnation began in a small way in an obscure village, may it remind us that small beginnings are never insignificant. May we ourselves commit our lives to You as Your spirit enters our hearts and lives. Let each of us continue to be a point of beginning anew for Your love in the world. As we prepare on this Christmas Eve to celebrate the birth of Your Son among us, may we express to You our sense of deep abiding joy and thanksgiving for such love. For it is in the name of Jesus Christ, our we pray. Amen.

CHRISTMAS DAY SUNDAY

Loving God, we bow before the mystery of this special day. This day is enveloped with the surprising way you came into our world through the birth of a baby by a young maiden in a small, obscure town named Bethlehem. The depth of your divine love to come quietly and uniquely in the form of a baby astounds us. The mystery of your incarnation evades our understanding, interpretation, and words to grasp the surprising physical way you chose to enter our world. We know that many will strive to probe the meaning of your incarnation, but the best minds of all persons, including scholars and theologians, will never fully grasp such a unique event.

The personal depth of your love and grace in the face of our sins draws us to your presence. We know we cannot deserve or earn such love, so, we acknowledge our thanksgiving and recommit ourselves to serving you more faithfully. May we not let the merriment and family festivities of this day cause us to lose sight of the real meaning of the birth of Your Son. May we allow our celebration of this day most of all to focus on the wonder and mystery of the birth of Your Son.

As we reflect on the transforming power of Your love in the birth of Your Son, may that awareness cause us to dedicate our lives not only to celebrating the birth of Your Son, but to sharing that love with those who have not personally experienced such love. Humbly, we express our gratitude this Sunday for the birth of Your Son. In the name of Jesus Christ, whose birth we celebrate. Amen.

Sunday After Christmas

O loving God, we have now taken our yearly journey to Bethlehem, but many of us are tired from lives that have been too busy and too cluttered. Did You mean for us to celebrate Your Son's birth in that way? Surely You intended for Your Son's birth to bring us peace, joy and renewal, and a sense of togetherness, of being in touch with life's deepest mysteries and realities. Grant that sorting through the debris of Christmas, we may find that sense of being in touch and may breathe easier knowing that You are at work in the world, continuing to become Incarnate in the acts of love and fellowship begun in Your Son Jesus Christ.

As we near the end of another year, we pray that world peace may find root in honest desire and grow into an atmosphere of trust and goodwill among men and women around the world. We pause today to remember the poor and homeless and ask if we may find ways to feed and house them. We remember the sick that they may receive healing. We pray for the grieving that their hearts may be comforted, for the lonely that they may find relationships that help, for the fearful that they may be given confidence, for the doubtful that they may have faith, and for the cynical that they may experience trust, for all children and young people that they may be kept from harmful ways until they are wise enough to meet the temptations that confront them.

Grant to Your church courage, strength, and endurance. Help us to covet Your leadership above riches, powers, and earthly approval. Teach us how to find You in quietness and follow You in faithfulness. We shall praise You with the angels forever and ever. Through Jesus Christ, our living Lord, we pray. Amen.

GENERAL PASTORAL PRAYERS

Eternal God, Shepherd of Our Soul, your Spirit knows us better than we know ourselves. Make us then aware of attitudes that are hurtful to our neighbors. Forgive our gossip that we may know the meaning of thoughtfulness. Forgive our fault-finding so we may know the meaning of friendship. Forgive our bitterness that we may know the meaning of joy. Forgive our bigotry that we may know the meaning of brotherhood. Help us to remember attitudes that are hurtful to our own families.

Deny us anger that we may know the meaning of self-control. Deny us miserliness that we may know the meaning of generosity. Deny us pettiness that we may know the meaning of greatheartedness. Deny us cowardice that we may know the meaning of courage. Deny us hardness that we may know the meaning of forgiveness.

Help us to remember attitudes that are hurtful to ourselves. Overcome our self-centeredness that we may know the meaning of freedom. Overcome our self-righteousness so that we may know the meaning of faith. Overcome our quick judgement of others that we may know the meaning of understanding. Overcome our despair that we may know the meaning of hope. Overcome our hate that we may know the meaning of love. Overcome our fears that we may know the meaning of peace. As we pray it in the name of Jesus Christ, the living Lord. Amen.

GENERAL

Eternal Father, we confess that we have often stormed Your gates in so many emergencies and moments of desperation. Now on this quiet Sunday, let us sense Your presence and sustaining power. Some of us here have experienced the storms of grief and our feelings are low, so we pray that You will warm our hearts with the embrace of Your Spirit. We confess that life seems so perplexing with all of its accidents and pain, the hand of death on some in the prime of life, the lingering of those who are helplessly senile, the loss of the young and innocent in war. We confess that we sometimes feel pain and suffer depression and are acquainted with sorrow. We are frustrated and weary with praying that war will come to an end. War seems to continue in one place or the other. We pray for peace.

We have to confess, Lord, that we simply do not understand much of life. But like a small child we reach out our hand to feel the grasp of Yours upon ours. May Your grasp uphold us. Touch us now. We await further light but continue to lean upon You in humble trust. Let each of us now in this place hear Your voice as it calls us by name and touches our individual needs. Where there is discouragement and we feel low, pick us up and make us useful again. When sin has overwhelmed us, strengthen us. When pride has distorted our estimate of ourselves, touch us to see ourselves through Your eyes. Watch beside the beds of pain of those who suffer. And, Lord, if we think too low of ourselves remind us that we have been created by your hand.

Open our eyes to the possibilities of what we and Your church can be as we rededicate ourselves to you. Help each of us to become the kind of Christian Church that will help Your kingdom to come and Your will to be done on this earth as it is in heaven. Teach us how to reach across racial and any other barriers that keep us from serving You. Guide us as we work for the unity of Your church with our brothers and sisters on this day and in the days to come. Through Christ, our example and Lord, we pray. Amen.

Prayer Of Intercession

Eternal God, It is in the mystery of communion with Christ that we pray for the Church throughout the world, praying in particular for the places where our church has done mission work in the past or will do in the coming year like Goldsboro, Henderson, Mississippi, Louisiana, NYC, Honduras, Kiev, Helena, India, and other places.

We pray for the people in this community of faith and all who are touched by its ministry in this city through our ministries like Weekday Preschool, clothing ministry, AIDS Care Team, Wake Interfaith Hospitality Network, Meals on Wheels, Angel Tree, Homeless Bags, Prayer Shawls, our Sunday School, music and children, youth, mission programs, and many others.

We pray for the sick, the bereaved, our homebound members, the oppressed, lonely, confused, and the homeless in our city and nation. Guide us to concrete and lasting ways to continue helping these particular needs. We pray in particular this morning for direction in our nation's financial crisis, for guidance in casting our vote for our new president and other political leaders next month.

We pray for the broken and torn fabric of the earth as it yearns for healing, praying in particular for an end soon to the ongoing wars in Iraq and Afghanistan, for the persons suffering from war, drought, famine, or genocide in countries like India, Zimbabwe, Ethiopia, Sudan, and Darfur.

And because you are one with us, O Christ, enable us to share your life with the world by sharing our own lives with the world. As we commune at your Table, may we sense your presence. As we eat the bread and drink from the cup, we open our spirit to your Spirit. Feed our soul to be renewed within. We eat this bread and drink this cup in memory of Christ's suffering and death. This sacrificial love is beyond our understanding. We bow in gratitude for such grace. And so, we pray, in the words you have taught us: Our Father who art in heaven....

GENERAL

Eternal Father, too often we come huffing and puffing into your presence. Life is often so busy, and we are so rushed that we seldom have time to prepare ourselves for worship. Slow us down in this hour that we might be still and know that You are here.

Slow us down so that we can realize our own needs and confess them to You and sense Your forgiveness. Slow us down so that we might hear those around us who have needs. Slow us down to realize the needs of our own church so that we can respond as You would have us commit our lives.

But, oh Lord, we also pray that You will speed us up. Speed us up into deeper commitments into Your way. Speed us up in sacrificial giving. Speed us up in sacrificial living. Speed us up, oh Lord, to do the work that You have called us to do; to share the good news of Christ with others.

We come this morning, oh Lord, to pause, to hear Your voice and then to rise from this place and go out and serve in Your name. Give us the courage, the wisdom, and the power to share Your grace with others. Through Christ who gave his all for us we pray. Amen.

GENERAL

Eternal God, Our Father, You have loved us for all eternity. We are conscious that we live in a world created by Your spirit. You are aware that it will take eye, ear, heart, and the totality of our being for us to live in this world. So, grant that we will commit our lives fully to You so that we might find our rightful place as Your servants.

We are conscious also that we live in a very busy world. Sometimes our busyness keeps us from serving You effectively. Our busyness at home sometimes keeps us from hearing the needs of those around us. Our concerns about those things outside of our home cause us not to hear their needs. May we listen to our wives or husbands or children or other members of our family. Enable us to know how to attune our lives so that we can learn to be responsive and seek to meet these needs. Sometimes our busyness in our jobs distracts us from doing our work, as we should. We pray that we will learn not simply to bury ourselves in busyness but to find the meaning of life and why we are here as people.

We confess also that sometimes our busyness within our church keeps us from being about Your real work in the world. We become so distracted with trivialities and keeping things straight and orderly that we have missed our calling to be Your children in the world. Enable us, we pray, to sense what Your real work is all about as we seek to love and serve You effectively.

We see change all around us in the world, but we confess that we do not really like change very much. Forgive us when we resist new ideas, new thoughts, and new ways. Grant, Oh God, that we may not seek so much to cling to the past as to be open and responsive to the freedom of Your spirit, which can come in such a variety of ways. We bring to you now those in our church family who are ill, who have heavy burdens or who are grieving. Sustain them with Your shepherding grace. Touch our spirits now as we open them unto You. Through Jesus Christ, our eternal Lord, we pray. Amen.

GENERAL

Eternal God, we confess that we do not always understand the mystery of Your presence. We come acknowledging we cannot always see You clearly. We confess that sometimes this may be because we are looking in the wrong places and not at the right time or in the right way. We want to know You, love You and understand You.

We are told that You are in the night and in the day; in the sun and in the rain; in the good and in the bad; in the brightness and in the darkness; sadness and joy. Teach us, Lord, how to see You wherever Your spirit is.

May all of creation point to You. May we learn to see You, as the ancient psalmist did, in the flowers and the mountains, in the streams and in the valleys, in plenty and in need, in our family and in the faces of strangers. Speak to us in the ordinary moments of our living.

Speak to us through our work. Speak to us in this fellowship today so that we may sense Your presence among us. Open our eyes that we might see Your presence wherever it is. Forgive us when our mind, heart and eyes are closed so we are not able to see.

Bathe us anew now in the refreshing fountain of Your love. Cleanse us, refresh us, and direct us to serve You more fully. As we pray in the name of Jesus Christ, our living Lord. Amen.

GENERAL

Eternal God, we rejoice to be back in this place of beauty to lift our voices in praise to you and affirm our commitment to serving you faithfully. Thank you for all those through the years who have enabled us to gather as your people in this sacred place. Help us always to focus on you and your abundant grace as we gather here.

We come today aware that we have not made ourselves and we really cannot keep ourselves nor forgive ourselves, so we reach out to you. We thank you for your creation, our preservation, and redemption. We thank you for the wonderful challenge of living and for the opportunity of becoming your children. Teach us how to grow and to be nurtured in our faith.

We thank you for this church and for its commitment to service, teaching, love, and as your witness in this community. We come this day also acknowledging those in our fellowship who have grief, who have experienced illness, have known accidents, hardships, or pain. We ask you to sustain them.

Open our eyes as we come to this place that we might sense your strong presence. Open our ears so that we might hear the sounds of your presence. Open our hearts that we might feel your presence. Open our minds that we might think your thoughts after you. We come today searching to love you with our total being. Through Jesus Christ our Lord, we pray. Amen.

GENERAL

O God, we speak to You from the secret places of our soul. Deep calls to deep within us. We pray that You will walk beside us with Your presence and uphold us with Your strong arm. Guide us with Your direction. We pray that You will hear our aches, hear our joys, touch our fears, and touch our hopes, see our sorrows, and see our happiness, taste our remorse, and inspire our confidence.

We acknowledge our need for Your grace and presence today and ask that You forgive us for not listening to others, for jumping to conclusions too quickly and criticizing others needlessly, for not trying to understand and carry on Your work. O God, we want to care and help. Teach us Your way.

We want to celebrate the assurance of Your love, the abiding joy in Your presence, and the wonder of Your redemption. Having received so much, teach us through the example of Christ how to live lovingly, generously, faithfully, joyfully, and sacrificially. Through Jesus Christ our Lord, we pray. Amen.

GENERAL

Loving Father, we gather in this sacred place to praise Your name. We praise You for Your creation, love, grace, mercy, providence, and redemption. We know that we are not deserving of such love, but You seek us out with that love, even when we are disobedient and have turned away from you. Thank You for such amazing grace.

Bless all those who gather here for worship-young and old, singles and married, children and adults. We commit ourselves to You.

We pause in this hour to learn more about You and how we can serve You more effectively. In this quietness, we open our heart, mind, ears, and eyes so that we might sense Your presence among us. We bow in worship to adore Your name. We bring You our personal burdens and the burdens of our church family with the assurance of Your sustaining presence. Thank You for such love.

We come confessing our sins and seeking Your forgiveness. Thank You for loving us and forgiving us. We thank You for such amazing grace which cleanses us from all of our sins. In the name of Jesus Christ, in whom we have seen Your love supremely revealed, we pray. Amen.

GENERAL

Eternal Lord of our souls, there are so many things that we would like to have made new in our lives today. Some of us would like to have our health made new. We long to be strong and vigorous again. Some of us would like to have our love made new, to care for others the way we once did and feel that they care for us as they once did. Some of us would like to have our faith made new, to believe as we once believed; to feel the energizing power of that belief extending to everything we do and are.

Some of us would like to have our hope made new, to expect that good things are going to happen and that we are going to be rewarded by the future. Some of us would like to have our opportunities made new, to be able to start over again in our jobs, school, marriages, church, with our children, or with our parents. Some of us long to do things differently this time.

You are the God of all newness, Lord. You are the One who makes all things new and creates a new heaven and a new earth. So set newness in our heart-- new health, and new opportunities. Show us what it is to have new hopes, new visions, and new faith. Show us what it is to be born again, this time from above.

Anoint us with Your spirit's power. Lead us out of our old ways, and save us from everything that has grown old, cold, and repetitious. Give us life in Your Son and let us share that life with the world. As we pray in his strong name. Amen.

GENERAL

Eternal God, so often we have thought that to survive in today's world that we must keep our feelings to ourselves, play it cool, and keep the fences high. Help us to open our spirit to Your Spirit. Teach us what it means to be embraced by Your love, accepted by Your grace, strengthened by Your strong arms, and nurtured by Your presence. In this house of prayer, we want to learn how to be real, open, honest, and understood. So, teach us today.

Down inside some of us confess that we carry a brokenness that is too deep for telling. Some of us are madly in love with a past that can never be again. Some of us are tied to an image of ourselves that no longer exists. We feel that we are not loveable, yet You love us. We thank You for loving us. Love us still.

Love us until our conflicts are resolved. Love us until our broken spirits are healed. Love us until our perverseness is straightened. Love us until our sins lose their appeal. Love us until our darkness changes to light. Love us until our vision is Your vision of the kingdom that You have prepared for us. We open ourselves in this hour to be loved by Your presence. Through Jesus Christ our Lord, in whom we have seen this love, we pray. Amen.

GENERAL

Here we are in church again, Eternal Father. Some of us are here because of habit; some out of deep need; some for the joy of worship, and some are simply not sure why. We thank You for the church, We thank You for all of its strengths, its great heritage, sacrifice, service, guidance, moral leadership, and the proclamation of the Good News.

We are also aware of its weaknesses. We know that it is often more than it reveals and sometimes less than it says, but not nearly what it can be in the power of Christ. Strengthen Your church in its work. Enable us where we are weak to become stronger, We acknowledge that sometimes Your church is weak because of weak leaders, apathy, poor planning, and strategy that is not adaptive enough or sometimes too adaptive. Help those of us who claim to be Your special people not to feel privileged and selfish but aware of our responsibility to share this good news with others to love and serve, and to live in Your image.

We pause to thank you for the 68 years of ministry of Westover Baptist Church. We thank you for the service and dedication of the many lay persons and pastors who have served faithfully through these years. On this anniversary Sunday of our church, challenge us to recommit ourselves to your service and the rebuilding of our church to serve you more fully.

Thank You for Christ who is head of the church. May we love him and his church more. May we come to understand why Christ was willing to die for the church. Make us, o God, at least willing live for Your church and our Lord. In whose name we pray. Amen.

GENERAL

We come now to praise You, our Father, but we are caught so keenly in the awareness that our words are often insufficient and even insincere. Yet we are also aware that Your word teaches us that Your spirit still loves and cares for us. We cannot understand it. We are overwhelmed by the greatness of Your love and the mystery of it. We thank You for it.

We are aware that our words fall short of proclaiming our worship and our praise and our adoration. We acknowledge that our worship is mixed with insincerity, a sense of artificiality and unreality. Teach us how to worship, how to know what it means to feel and to sense and to know Your spirit. May we seek to find it even in this hour.

We come to acknowledge that so often we think we are self-made people. Teach us how really contingent, how dependent we are on You, and upon so many others. We come often saying that we are responsible people and reasonable people and yet we are aware often how unreasonable and irresponsible we are and how many blind spots there are within our lives, how much prejudice still overwhelms us and overshadows our thinking and distorts us and twists us into being that which we really do not want to be.

Sometimes we think that we are really free people, but make us aware of our bondage, our bondage to the flesh and our bondage to sin, our bondage to material things and our bondage to so many others around us. Teach us what it means to become free when we have become free in Your spirit.

So often we think we are alive to life and yet we come confessing that so much of the length and height, depth, and breadth of life itself we have really missed. We come now this day listening for that word from You, the word that imparts Your message to us of the coming of the gift of Yourself. So come now, breathe upon us and within us and through us Your word that we might know what it is to meet You in this hour, as we come listening in the name of Jesus Christ, our living Lord. Amen.

GENERAL

O God, we speak to You from the secret places of our soul. Deep calls to deep within us. We pray that You will walk beside us with Your presence and uphold us with Your strong arm. Guide us with Your direction. We pray that You will hear our aches, hear our joys, touch our fears, and touch our hopes, see our sorrows, and see our happiness, taste our remorse, and inspire our confidence.

We acknowledge our need for Your grace and presence today and ask that You forgive us for not listening to others, for jumping to conclusions too quickly and criticizing others needlessly, for not trying to understand and carry on Your work. O God, we want to care and help. Teach us Your way.

We want to celebrate the assurance of Your love, the abiding joy in Your presence, and the wonder of Your redemption. Having received so much, teach us through the example of Christ how to live lovingly, generously, faithfully, joyfully, and sacrificially. Through Jesus Christ our Lord, we pray. Amen.

GENERAL

Eternal God, we come today aware that we have not made ourselves and we really cannot keep ourselves nor forgive ourselves, so we reach out to you. We thank you for your creation, our preservation, and redemption. We thank you for the wonderful challenge of living and for the opportunity of becoming your children. Teach us how to grow and to be nurtured in our faith.

We thank you for this church and for its commitment to service, teaching, love, and as your witness in this community. We come this day also acknowledging those in our fellowship who have grief, who have experienced illness, have known accidents, hardships, or pain. We ask you to sustain them.

Open our eyes as we come to this place that we might sense your strong presence. Open our ears so that we might hear the sounds of your presence. Open our hearts that we might feel your presence. Open our minds that we might think your thoughts after you. We come today searching to love you with our total being. Through Jesus Christ our Lord, we pray. Amen

GENERAL

O God of every time and place, we thank you for the assurance that you are with us at this particular time, in this particular place. Some of us come this morning with our lives filled with great joy and enthusiasm for our jobs and friends. We are excited about our lives; our family life is good and our whole life seems to swell with a sense of radiance.

Others come this morning, dear Lord, for whom life is difficult and their burdens are heavy. They have experienced loneliness or depression, or anxiety, or fear, or sickness, or pain or other physical problems. So, this morning, we pray that your spirit will nourish them and sustain them. We pray that whatever our needs are this day we shall bring them to you with the assurance that you hear us and that you sustain us.

As we come to church this morning, give us the assurance that you are a living Lord who can minister to whatever our needs are. We know that you are a Lord who cleanses us from our sins, forgives us for our wrongdoings and guides us into the tomorrows. We thank you for Christ, who by his life, teachings, and death, demonstrated to us the power of service and sacrifice. Enable us, O Father, to follow his example as we seek to live and serve you in the world. Through Jesus Christ, our living Lord, we pray. Amen.

Selected Prayer

My prayer this morning is prayed in the words of Francis of Assisi (1182-1226) in his The Canticle of Brother Sun.

O most high, almighty, good Lord God, to you belong praise, glory, honor, and all blessing.

Praised be my Lord God with all his creatures and specially our brother the sun, who brings us the day and who brings us light; fair is he and shines with a very great splendor. O Lord, he shows us you.

Praised be my Lord for our sister the moon, and for the stars, which he has set clear and lovely in the heavens.

Praised be my Lord for our brother the wind, and for air and cloud, calms, and all weather by which you uphold life in all creatures.

Praised be my Lord for our sister water, who is very serviceable unto us, and humble and precious and clean.

Praised be my Lord for our brother fire, through whom you give us light in the darkness; and he is bright and pleasant and very strong.

Praised be my Lord for our mother the earth, who sustains us and keeps us and brings forth diverse fruits and flowers of many colors, and grass.

Praised be my Lord for all those who pardon one another for his love's sake, and who endure weakness and tribulation. Blessed are they who peaceably shall endure.

Praised be my Lord for our sister the death of the body, from which no man escapes.

Blessed are those who are found walking by your most holy will.

Praise and bless the Lord; and give thanks to him; and serve him with great humility. Amen.

General

Eternal God, we pause now to take time to speak with You. We confess that often we are so busy rushing from one thing to another, coming and going, walking, and running, so that we will not waste time, and consequently, we seldom have time for You.

Excuse us God, we are just too busy. We haven't time. We have just so much to do. We would like to pray, but we can't think, read, or wait. We haven't time. We are too busy. We know You understand. Life for us, O God, is filled with busyness. There is a child who is busy playing. He has no time now; later on, he says. There is a student at school, she has homework to do, no time now. Later on. There is a young man who has sports. He has no time now, but later on he says. There is the father who must play golf. He has no time now, later on he says. There is a mother with her club. No time now she says, later on. There are grandparents who have no time now for their grandchildren. Later on, they say. O God, there are those who are ill. They haven't time. There are those who are dying, but it is too late for them. They have no more time.

Forgive us, Lord, for wasting time, for killing time, and for using time so foolishly. Teach us to accept time as a great gift from You. May we sense that it is a perishable gift that will not keep. Teach us how to learn to wait upon You. We are aware that we only have the time which is given to us by You now. The years, the months and weeks, the days, the hours, and the minutes of our lives are all a gift from You. They are ours to fill quickly, calmly, and fully.

Teach us to learn to wait upon You so that we can learn to live life in its fullest. Let it begin now as we pause to listen to Your spirit in this hour. We come waiting upon You. Through Jesus Christ, our Lord, we pray. Amen.

General

Loving Father, we gather in this sacred place to praise Your name. We praise You for Your creation, love, grace, mercy, providence, and redemption. We know that we are not deserving of such love, but You seek us out with that love, even when we are disobedient and have turned away from you. Thank You for such amazing grace.

Bless all those who gather here for worship -- young and old, singles and married, children and adults. We commit ourselves to You. We pause in this hour to learn more about You and how we can serve You more effectively. In this quietness, we open our heart, mind, ears, and eyes so that we might sense Your presence among us. We bow in worship to adore Your name. We bring You our personal burdens and the burdens of our church family with the assurance of Your sustaining presence. Thank You for such love.

O Loving God, we confess that sometimes following You is not easy. It is hard to love you when even our own families and friends do not understand or support us. But teach us, Lord, to be loyal to You and to love You. Give us the courage to bear witness for Christ wherever we are. Give us strength in this hour to love and serve you more faithfully.

We come confessing our sins and seeking Your forgiveness. Thank You for loving us and forgiving us. We thank You for such amazing grace which cleanses us from all of our sins. In the name of Jesus Christ, in whom we have seen Your love supremely revealed, we pray. Amen.

General

Loving Father, we gather in this sacred place to praise Your name. We praise You for Your creation, love, grace, mercy, providence, and redemption. We know that we are not deserving of such love, but You seek us out with that love, even when we are disobedient and have turned away from you. Thank You for such amazing grace.

Bless all those who gather here for worship -- young and old, singles and married, children and adults. We commit ourselves to You.

We pause in this hour to learn more about You and how we can serve You more effectively. In this quietness, we open our heart, mind, ears, and eyes so that we might sense Your presence among us. We bow in worship to adore Your name. We bring You our personal burdens and the burdens of our church family with the assurance of Your sustaining presence. Thank You for such love.

We come confessing our sins and seeking Your forgiveness. Thank You for loving us and forgiving us. We thank You for such amazing grace which cleanses us from all of our sins. In the name of Jesus Christ, in whom we have seen Your love supremely revealed, we pray. Amen.

General

Lord God of life, hope, and joy, breathe your spirit upon us and our very hopes. Enable us to feel the strength and the power of your breath and the possibilities that are within us. May we sense your guidance and your power in all that we seek to undertake.

Throw open the windows of our lives and let the breeze of your spirit rush in and overcome our stale thinking, so that we can have new hopes, new dreams, and new possibilities. Blow over those fences in our lives which have surrounded us and kept us from going in new directions, undertaking new goals, or seeking new ways of ministry. By the power of your grace knock these fences down and move us forward.

Remove blinders from our eyes that keep us from seeing those around us who have needs and sorrows, those who ache, who are hungry, tired, weary, frustrated, disillusioned, depressed, and hopeless. Breathe within us the breath of your joy which will be so overwhelming that we will want to share it with others. Well up within us that living water which comes from Jesus Christ our Lord. May this stream of water be so powerful within us that it will become a rushing stream that will flow through our lives and touch others to quench their needs.

Free us from the shackles which bind us to the past, to bad habits and broken dreams. Open our eyes this day to what we can become through Jesus Christ who suffered and died for us and lives again. For we offer this prayer in his strong name. Amen.

General

Eternal Father, we come now to worship you. But we come confessing that we do not always find it easy. We spend so much of our time playing hideandseek with you. Your spirit comes seeking us and we hide from you in our T.V. sets, newspapers, play, work, and sometimes even in our worship. Break in upon us in our worship this hour with the reality of your presence and don't let us settle for worship, which is ordinary, routine, and mediocre, or casual. May the power of your presence be so strong and real within our minds and hearts that our faith will come alive with meaning, with power and strength, love, hope, and courage.

O God, teach us to hate evil and to love the good, to be willing to take the hard and difficult way when it is your way and not the easy path when it is the popular or softer way. Forgive us for not trying when the way is hard, and the obstacles are difficult. May we remember the crucified way of Christ. Give us then courage to take up our crosses and follow him in the war against evil, in the battle of truth over ignorance, justice over inequity, and righteousness over corruption. Help us, O God, to bring light where there is darkness, hope where there is fear, concern where there is apathy, victory where there is defeat, and redemption where there is division.

Guide us to draw upon the strength of your abiding presence which can enable us to become what you have created us to be. Let

us not grow weary then in welldoing. Inspire us with confidence
to continue to follow the way of Christ wherever it leads us. For
we pray it in his strong name. Amen.

General

Eternal God, sometimes we confess that we too feel forsaken
like our Lord. We feel forsaken, abandoned, isolated and alone.
There are times when we want to scream: "God, where are
you?" You seem so far removed from us, so silent to our needs,
so unconcerned, so remote, so distant. Our agonies and burdens
press down upon us, and you do not seem available or concerned.
You are so far removed from us that we want to cry rivers of tears.
Sometimes we simply want to whisper. We long to whisper our
concerns, hopes, and dreams to know that you hear and that you
care.

O God, we do not want this distance to be between us. Is it
of our own making? Is it something that we have done? Show us
your nearness, your available presence. Forgive us, O God, for the
sin which always separates us from you.

May we learn from our own Lord's suffering and agony that
you are always present and near to us, seeking to meet our needs
even when we do not know it. We open ourselves now like fertile
soil to let your spirit rain the love of your grace upon us. Bathe us
in the sunshine of your radiant love. May our spirits grow warm
as they are embraced by your presence this hour. Through Jesus
Christ our living Lord, we pray. Amen.

General

Eternal God, many of us come to you today thirsty. We thirst
for recognition, love, acceptance, hope and meaning. Satisfy that
thirst through your grace. Forgive us, O God, for not responding
to the thirst we see around us in others. Forgive us for not caring.
May we be sensitive and responsive to the needs of others. May

we reach out with a cup of cold water in your name to minister to others.

Fill our lives with a strong desire to care. Forgive us, Lord, when we have turned a harsh and deaf ear to those in need. For those of us who have experienced your forgiveness, teach us how to forgive. Fill us this day with the cooling, satisfying, refreshing water of your Spirit. In the thirst of whatever dark night we have, may we know that you are there with us. Help us to thirst after righteousness in such a way that we will have satisfaction. Bless those on this day who thirst with pains of illness and sorrow. Satisfy them with your presence. We come today through Jesus Christ, who is the living Water. Amen.

General

Eternal Father, you have taught us to hunger and thirst after you. We confess today that we wish we really did hunger and thirst after you as much as we do for food and drink. But most of us simply do not. Too often we are satisfied only to admire Christ and not really follow him. Make us aware that we need more than just a snack of faith when you have given us a whole banquet. Sometimes we wonder why we grow fat when we overeat physical food and cannot understand why we stay so lean spiritually when we seldom eat of the spiritual meat and potatoes of the gospel. Make us aware that our spiritual muscles cannot grow strong without use and exercise. Teach us how to use them daily and weekly as we open ourselves to you.

We confess that our minds are often filled with thoughts and ideas that reflect too much of the profane world. Cleanse us with the scrubbing power of your forgiving grace. Touch us with the purity of your love. Lift us from low goals to mountaintop ideas and fill us with desires for selfless living. Nourish our lives with your penetrating love just as our earth is nourished by rain, snow, and sunshine.

Make us alive to your world like a small child. Give us a spirit of excitement and a sense of discovery. Give us a new sense of adventure. May the wonder of every bush and tree and snowflake and star and floating cloud remind us of you. May we be childlike as we wait before you. Through Christ, we pray. Amen.

General

O God of Love and Grace, We gather in this sacred place to open our mind and heart to Your Spirit. We acknowledge that our pride and arrogance often block our entrance into Your Presence. Forgive us for assuming too much, expecting so little, speaking instead of listening, taking instead of giving, demanding instead of serving, apathetic instead of caring, tight fisted instead of openhanded, callous instead of gentle, closed minded instead of being open minded, unbelieving instead of trusting and prayer less instead of prayerful.

May we open our spirits to Your divine Spirit that we might feel the exhilarating breath of Your Presence and the nurturing direction of Your Spirit. We really do want to be led, to be better people, more loving, gracious, helpful, serving and more like the Lord we worship. So, we come to this place today for that guidance. May we feel the touch of Your Presence as You enter our inner chamber to give us light on our pathway to follow Your way to become genuine children of Your Kingdom. May that touch be so real that we cannot leave this place without the assurance that You are indeed directing our pathway. Amen.

General

Eternal God, we thank you for your abundant love which we have seen in the sacrifice of Christ. Thank you for that love. We open our hearts to you and acknowledge our own weaknesses and sins. O God, we confess that we are so guilty of the sin of judging falsely and with such quick unsupportable information. Thank you, God, for not judging us by our sins but by your grace.

Having experienced such marvelous grace, teach us to see ourselves through your eyes. Watch beside the beds of pain of those who suffer. And, Lord, if we think too lowly of ourselves remind us that we have been created by your hand.

Thank you for loving us in spite of our sins. We confess our sins to you and seek to receive your grace. Through Christ who died for us, we pray. Amen.

General

Creator God, we acknowledge that too often we go through life with downcast eyes and tight lips. We are often sullen and afraid. We pray that You will come this day and surprise us with the joy of Your presence. We come to this place of worship seeking to be remade in Your image. We pray today for those whose lives are met by difficulties. We pray for those who are in the hospital and their life is slipping away in a matter of hours, days, or weeks. We pray for those who are forced to move or retire from the work and places they have known and loved. We pray for those who have recently moved to our own community and as they adjust to a new situation. We pray for those who are met by unusual deadlines, and they are unsure which way to turn or how to meet them. O Lord, make us sensitive to those 'who feel such pressures and may we reach out to them with love and care. We pray for those in the war in the gulf and the families who are separated from them. May peace come to that region of the world soon.

We pray for ourselves. Yet we are ashamed that we have often done so little with so much. We struggle to be obedient to Your way, yet we know we are not very obedient at all. Give us a keen sense of Your presence. Give us also a keener sense of self understanding. May it be so keen that we shall be able to sense and hear Your presence especially with us at this hour. May we learn to think of ourselves not too highly or too lowly but as You would have us see ourselves as Your own children. Give us the sense of what is vital in life, lest we waste our life by giving our attention to trifles. Give us respect for all people even as You have given Your Son to redeem all persons. We acknowledge that You are the Lord and Creator of all the earth. Surround us now in this place with Your presence. May our worship be real as we come in the name of Jesus Christ our living Lord.

O God, we thank you that you do not always give us what we ask for. We acknowledge that some of our requests are vain and selfish. We thank you for responding to us according to our needs. Lord, help us to accept your grace and be willing to live as you would have us live. Through Christ, who lived, died, and gave us an example in how to pray and live. Amen.

General

Eternal Father, we confess that we have often stormed your gates in so many emergencies and moments of desperation. Now on this quiet Sunday, let us sense your presence and sustaining power. Some of us here have experienced the storms of grief and our feelings are low, so we pray that you will warm our hearts with the embrace of your spirit. We confess that life seems so perplexing with all of its accidents and pain, the hand of death on some in the prime of life, the lingering of those who are helplessly senile, the loss of the young and innocent in war. We confess that we sometimes feel pain and suffer depression and are acquainted with sorrow. We are frustrated and weary with praying that war will come to an end. War seems to continue in one place or the other. We pray for peace.

We have to confess, Lord, that we simply do not understand much of life. But like a small child we reach out our hand to feel the grasp of yours upon ours. May your grasp uphold us. Touch us now. We await further light but continue to lean upon you in humble trust. Let each of us now in this place hear your voice as it calls us by name and touches our individual needs. Where there is discouragement and we feel low, pick us up and make us useful again. When sin has overwhelmed us, strengthen us. When pride has distorted our estimate of ourselves teach us how, O Lord, to reach out with grace toward others.

Open our eyes to the possibilities of what we and your church can be as we rededicate ourselves to you. Help each of us to become the kind of Christian that will help your kingdom to come and your will to be done on this earth as it is in heaven. Through Christ, our example and Lord, we pray. Amen.

General

O God, we confess that too often we want to read about Your teachings, discuss them, debate them, and sometimes even argue about them. But seldom do we really want to live them. We know Your high values got You in trouble, Lord, and we don't want trouble. So, we avoid or ignore many of Your teachings.

O Lord, teach us to know that if we would truly follow You that the way sometimes is hard but the end which we achieve will make our relationships with others radically different. May we follow Christ, our Lord, who is the example of all things in both living and dying. Amen.

Prayer For Peace

Eternal God, we confess today that our spirits are caught up in the war in the Middle East. We pray that Your grace will guide this war to an early conclusion. We pray for an early peace. We pray that Your spirit will be with all persons involved. Give them inner peace which is found in Your love and grace. We pray that soon this turmoil shall come to an end and that once again peace and justice will reign in the Middle East.

We pray now as we come into this time of worship that we might sense Your spirit among us. We confess that often we are confined in such narrow places and categories in our own minds and hearts that we cannot always see and sense Your presence. So, we come today praying that You will stretch our minds. Stretch them to see new opportunities and new ways of serving you.

Stretch our minds that we might grow in our faith and not be content with where we are presently in our spiritual pilgrimage. Stretch our hearts that we might be more compassionate and respond to the needs of those in our church, community, and around the world.

Stretch our hands so that we might reach out to those who have needs. Help us to become instruments to minister in a loving and caring way in Your name. Stretch our lives so that we might break free from any shackle that binds us to the past, apathy, or complacency and go forth in service for You. Teach us how to find ways to minister for You in this church and in this community that others might know Jesus Christ as Lord. Stretch our lives, O Lord, with the power of Your spirit. Set our hearts beating with the sense of Your strength that sustains and guides us in all that we do.

O God, we thank you that you do not always give us what we ask for. We acknowledge that some of our requests are vain and selfish. We thank you for responding to us according to our needs. Lord, help us to accept your grace and be willing to live as you would have us live. Through Christ, who lived, died, and gave us an example in how to pray and live. Amen.

General

O great God, Shepherd of our souls, we come this morning pausing to sense the power of Your presence among us, within us and around us. We come acknowledging that we have not created ourselves but are Your creation. We come acknowledging that often we wander off in our own pathways and move away from Your guidance and direction. So, we come back now to this holy place which is set apart for a meeting with You so we can sense Your presence and Your shepherding care.

We thank You for all of life. For the challenge of living, for the opportunity of being Your children to grow and to be nurtured by

You. We thank You for this church, for its commitment to service, and love in so many ways in our community.

We come now to this day acknowledging that there are those in our fellowship who bear burdens of illness. Some have experienced accidents or hardships, grief, or pain. We ask Your shepherding care for them. Sustain them, open their eyes so that they might sense Your presence.

Open our eyes and ears this day that we might see and hear the sound of Your presence as we come now to worship. May we leave this place assured that You are the Shepherd of our souls and that we will recommit ourselves to following Your leadership in all that we say and do. Through the name of Jesus Christ, the Good Shepherd, we pray. Amen.

General

Eternal God, we come to this place of worship because some of us simply must. There is something within us that draws us to this place. There is something within us that wants to do what is right, but we confess that we are often pulled down those paths that are base and sinful. Civil war seems to rage within us, and we are pulled in so many directions. We pray on this day that You will pull us unto Yourself. Let the embrace of Your presence make us warm within and strengthen us to recapture the joy of discipleship.

O loving God, we confess that sometimes we do feel low. Our eyes burn with the parade of problems that we see personally, nationally, and world-wide. Some of us here today need jobs, new opportunities and encouragement, better relationships at home, at work and even at play. The world conditions of poverty, disease, war, and pollution march across our vision, and they frighten and disturb us and sometimes challenge us. O Lord, help us not to give way to despair, but may we rise up with courage and faith to be a part of the creative force in the world to fight evil, poverty, and disease. Strengthen us to be the salt, light, and leaven in the world.

Give us now a faith that is alive and vital with enthusiasm, joy, and radiance. Make our faith alive with wonder, vitality, hope, optimism, and confidence, because we walk daily with You. May our love for You and the love we have experienced from Your great hand enable us to know how to love each other better. May this day the power of that love cause us to live and serve You in a way that will bring honor and glory to Your name. In the name of Jesus Christ, who taught us how to love, we pray. Amen.

General

Thank you, Eternal Father, for the power of your presence which can transform our lives. We come today seeking to love you with all our strength. Strengthen our minds on this day so that they might be open and developing and continuously growing as we search for truth. May we fear no intellectual challenge as we follow your spirit but walk unafraid in whatever lies before us.

Strengthen our hearts that we might love as you have loved us. Forgive us when we love in a narrow and confined way. Teach us to love the unlovable even as you have loved us when we have been unlovable.

Strengthen our hands so that we might reach out to those who need help along life's way. To those who have fallen into sin, help us to lift them up by your grace; to those who have fallen into doubts, give them renewed faith; to those who have fallen into grief, sustain them with your strong arms; to those who have fallen into loneliness and depression, strengthen them by your presence.

Strengthen our souls and lives so that they may be more fully open to your love and presence as we work, play and live. Be in our living and be in our worship this hour. O Lord stretch us and strengthen us with your dynamic presence. As we pray in the name of Jesus Christ our living Lord. Amen.

General

O God of all places and especially known in this place by so many through the years, we lift our spirits to commune with Your divine Spirit today. Give us a strong sensitivity to Your Presence. We long to be assured that You are with us today. Speak to our mind, stir our emotions, inspire our enthusiasm, encourage our service, direct our actions, motivate our thoughts, strengthen our moral fiber, and touch us with reassurance.

We acknowledge our failures and sins and ask for Your forgiveness and strength to withstand the temptations that whirl around us and within us. May the assurance of Your Presence today provide us strength to worship and serve You faithfully. Through Christ, we pray. Amen.

General

Eternal God, Creator of the entire universe and the source of all that is, we bow before Your Holy Presence. We marvel at the beauty of Your creation, especially in this fall season. The rain and the cooler weather remind us of the changing of nature. The slowly changing color of the leaves in the mountains also reminds us of the wonder and mystery of Your creation. We know that wintertime will be here soon, followed by spring, and the budding of new life will remind us of the beauty and continuous cycle of life.

We pause this day to pray for our country in this time of financial instability. Guide our leaders to find a sound policy to stabilize our economy. We pray for wisdom in casting our vote for the next President of the United States. Guide us individually and our nation as we vote and as we seek to meet this present financial crisis, Help us find the high moral and ethical ground on which to walk. Keep us from being quick to jump to criticism and judgment. Help all those who lead us in our government. Guide our public officials to the highest moral and personal standards of integrity as they lead our nation.

In the quietness of this sacred place, may we commit our lives more fully to knowing You, loving You, and serving You. We confess our sins, acknowledge our faults, and our disposition to selfishness. Forgive us for seeking easy answers to difficult problems and the willingness to take the low road instead of the high road.

As Your church, teach us how to love and support each other more, especially in times of difficulties, illness, and grief. May the love that we have experienced from Christ be reflected in our love and concern for each other. Forgive us when we become so concerned about our own ends and desires that we do not sense the concerns and needs of others around us. Thank You for sticking with us when we fail You so often. Teach us how to stick with others when they fail or struggle. We lift the empty cup of our spiritual life to You and pray that You will fill it full with the life-quenching water of Your Presence. Through Jesus Christ our Lord, we pray. Amen.

The Coming Of A New Pastor

We thank You for all the pastors and ministers and laypersons who have served You faithfully for almost two centuries in this church. As the church now awaits the coming of its new pastor, Chris Chapman, and the new chapter that will enfold with his coming, gird him and these good people with the confidence that You are present with them in this time of transition and new beginnings and will guide them in their ministry in the years ahead. Give them expectancy and hope, confidence and encouragement, enthusiasm and commitment, faith and assurance as this congregation and its new pastor begin their ministry together.

May minor differences be put aside as they move forward together in unity of purpose and commitment to serving Christ to the best of one's ability. Bless Chris, Dana, Ian and Margaret and this congregation with Your love and grace. May they begin a romance of ministry that will grow and blossom over the years. May this be a place where all who come will see the spirit of Christ in the manner, words, thoughts, and behavior of this church family. May the highest desire of all be to serve Christ and not for personal recognition or acclaim.

We pause this morning, O Lord, to pray for our new pastor, Chris Chapman, and his family. Bless them in this time of transition as they close the chapter of their ministry in Winston Salem and prepare to move here. As he comes, fill us with excitement and enthusiasm about our new beginning together. May we each dedicate ourselves to doing all we can to enable Chris to minister effectively among us for Christ's sake and the unity of our church. We make that commitment now with Your help.

I thank You for the privilege of serving as Pastor in the Interim for twenty months in this sacred place. I lift these good people to You in my prayer with confidence that they will continue to serve You faithfully here. I have sensed their love for Christ and his Church and for their desire to serve. Fortify that intent with Your constant Presence and guidance. Comfort us always with the assurance that nothing ever separates us from Your Presence. Through Christ who goes before us, we pray. Amen.

The Coming Of A New Pastor

Eternal God, we gather today to acknowledge a new chapter in the life of this congregation will begin soon. We thank you for all the dedicated service which has gone before us by former pastors, staff, and good lay people. This church has been blessed by them and we are grateful for their sacrifice of love.

As we look to the future, teach us how to serve you more faithfully, share the good news of Christ more easily with others, and bear the burdens of one another more cheerfully and to love each other more fully.

As this congregation looks to the future with a new Pastor, teach us how to get to know one another better and work together in your name and seek to grow in grace and knowledge of Christ. Bless Mary Mann and her family and the unique gifts they bring. May we love and support them as they begin their ministry with us. Help us to learn from one another, affirm the gifts we recognize in others and support each other with genuine love. Let this be a time of new beginnings, new visions, new hopes, and a time of forgiving old quarrels, hurts, gossip, or words of criticism. Knit us together as your children, bonded together in love, as we lean on Christ, the head of the Church.

Bless now those who are ill, grieving, lonely, or in distress. May your strong grace be real to them. We bow before you now in expectation. We know you are here. Help us to sense your presence. Amen.

First Sunday Of A New Pastor

Eternal God, we lift before you the members of this congregation as we begin a new pilgrimage together. We thank You for the rich heritage and dedicated ministry which has gone on in the past years and continues to this time. We know that You are present with us at this present moment. Give us the assurance of Your abiding presence and direction as we labor as pastor and people together. May we not be so bound by the past that we cannot see Your leadership for the future.

We commit this present time in worship to You. We come to fortify ourselves and to be strengthened to serve You more effectively. We give to You all the anxieties we have about the future and our uncertainties about the roads of life ahead of us individually and as a church. Our faith has been built on the confidence and assurance of Your presence with us in the past. We turn now and look toward the future. As a child trusts its parents, as the birds trust the air, the animals trust their instincts, so we lean in trust upon You and your grace.

Give us the assurance that Your strong arm will bear us up no matter what our difficulty is. We trust You whether our burden is grief, a family member who is ill, a family member who has lost a job, or we are crushed by a load of depression. May we have a strong sense of Your presence to lift us up.

As we step into the future before us, we open our spirits to Your Spirit so we might be led by Your hand; feel the strength of Your grace and love, and the breath of Your presence within us. Lord, we wait now in confidence for Your guidance in all that we think and do. We pray this in the name of Jesus Christ, our living Lord. Amen.

4.

PRAYERS
AT END OF SERMON

The prayer at the conclusion of the sermon might draw upon the central thrust of the sermon and encourage the worshipper to incorporate the lesson into one's life.

O loving God, we acknowledge that too often we model ourselves after the world of darkness and yet have not learned from them how to be more effective in our Christian work. Forgive us, teach us how to use our resources in serving and loving You more effectively. Through Christ we pray. Amen.

O Father, forgive us for clamoring for the chief seats, for wanting name recognition. Help us, O Lord, to be willing to serve faithfully, work humbly, give sacrificially, labor devotedly, and minister lovingly. May we give all the praise to you. Through Christ, who modeled service through his teaching, living, and dying. Amen.

Loving God, forgive us when we feel holier than others. Make us mindful that we are always sinners- sinners saved by grace- but sinners. We thank You for Your grace and atonement through Jesus Christ. We thank You for the gift of eternal life which we receive not by something we do but by Your loving us. Through Christ we pray. Amen.

O God, forgive us when we make your religion so stuffy that we fail to reveal the joy and gladness of our faith. Thank You,

Lord, for receiving us sinners all. Teach us to reach out to others with the same grace that we have known. Through Jesus Christ our redeeming Lord. Amen.

Eternal God, we acknowledge that our lips are so prone to make excuses. Forgive us. Help us, O Lord, rather than making excuses to be willing to turn to You and find redemption, grace, and guidance. We open our hearts and minds. Through Christ, who stands at the door and knocks, we pray. Amen.

Creator God, we thank You for honoring us with our work. May we do our very best to be co-laborers with You. Forgive us when we do not use the gifts which we have to our fullest ability. Thank You for entrusting us with opportunities to serve. May we minister with joy and gladness as we work in Your name. Amen.

O God, needs are all around us. Forgive us that we often close our eyes and refuse to see; or shut our ears and refuse to hear. Give us hands and feet that are willing to respond to the needs around us so that we might be neighbors to others wherever there is need. Through Christ we pray. Amen.

Eternal God, sometimes our sins seem overwhelming to us, and we acknowledge them. Sometimes we are blind to our sinfulness. Open our eyes to see our sins, and may we be willing to confess them and then arise and come to You that we might know forgiveness and grace. In the name of Jesus Christ, our Lord, who forgives us, we pray. Amen.

O Father, we thank you for Your grace that saves, loves, and makes us whole. We thank You for the opportunity to respond to Your love and say yes. Forgive us, Lord, for closing the door and not being willing to respond to Your grace. May we not hear you say, "I never knew you." But may we hear the words instead, "Enter into the joy of eternal life." Through Christ our Lord we pray. Amen.

O Lord God of eternity, we pause to thank You for the great gift of life and eternal life we have experienced through Christ. We seek to open our lives to Your grace. Give us the courage to respond by saying yes to Jesus Christ, our Lord. Amen.

O Father, many of us have wandered far from you and we are lost. Bring us home again. Give us healing and salvation that comes only through your grace. O God who seeks us, find us now, through Christ we pray. Amen.

Loving God, we confess today that Christ is the solid rock. Help us to build our lives upon him so that we can face whatever storms and difficulties beat upon the structure of our lives. Give us the grace within to stand and having done all to remain firm even into eternity. Through Christ we pray, Amen.

Eternal Father, we thank You for the Word that endures, and can change our lives, as it finds the place to grow within our hearts. We open them now to You. Help us to grow more like what you would have us be. Through Christ our Lord. Amen.

O Holy God, we know that our conversation with You is weak and inadequate. Our prayers are often just nods and winks at you. Few of us really attend, listen, or wait with expectancy, O Lord, teach us how to pray, Through Christ, who lived and died knowing how to pray, Amen.

All-encompassing God, we thank You for the inclusive nature of Your love which draws all persons to you. Forgive us, O God, for presuming that we can judge where another person is in his or her relationship with You. Teach us to be open like You. May each of us be concerned that he or she has given the life that we have to You. Amen.

Eternal Father. Give us a mustard seed faith. We are blind to so much of life and we have not learned to see at all. Forgive us for looking at life in such a negative way. Open our eyes to see the possibilities within us, around us and before us. Most of all, may we see the flaming power of Your spirit leading us forward through the difficult places of life. Amen.

Eternal God, we come acknowledging that too often we do cling too strongly to the old and to the familiar and are unwilling to let go and launch into the sea that is before us. Give us courage as Your people to hear Your voice and to be able to discern what is Your direction and what is our own. Through Christ we pray. Amen.

O God of life, the God who was, who is, and will always be, sustain us with the power of Your living presence. May we always live with hope, with a strong sense of your forgiveness, and the possibility of what we can be through Your grace and love. Amen.

O God of every time and place, and the God who is in this place now. speak to our hearts today. Open our ears and mind to Your spirit. May we see You, hear You, and respond. Direct us, O Lord, to give our hands in service according to the commission which we have received through our vision of Your love. In the name of the Christ, who taught us how to live and die. Amen.

O Lord God, strengthen us to wait upon You with courage and faith. Amen.

Eternal God, who speaks in so many ways, we thank You for speaking through ancient biblical stories. Continue to speak through our stories as we tell others how we have experienced You in our home, in our work, in our play, and at church. Continue to speak to us, O God, and may we pledge You our loyalty, as we seek to love and follow You as we have seen you supremely revealed through Christ. In his name we pray. Amen.

Father, forgive us for focusing our eyes so much upon ourselves that we cannot see the needs of others. Give to us a vision that will enable us to arise and serve You, as we follow Christ, whom we call Lord. Amen.

Father, forgive us for thinking You only speak through spectacular means. In this quiet moment, we open our life to let You nurture us. Bless our daily work, play, rest, and all that we do. May we sense You through all of life. May the ordinary events of all life become Your shrine. Through Christ we pray. Amen.

O God, who has revealed himself through Jesus Christ, and has loved us so much through his sacrificial death, give to us the desire to serve him faithfully. May the fire of your spirit set a flame burning within to live the Christlike life. May our hearts burn within us until we follow your guidance. For in his strong name, we pray. Amen.

O Loving God, like small children, we are so frightened of change. Teach us, Eternal Lord, in the midst of all of change that You are with us. May we learn to grow within change and through it. May Your spirit open new frontiers before us. As your pioneer people, may we be willing to march forward and not retreat, because we follow the banner of Christ who goes before us. Amen.

Gracious God, we thank You for the challenge of living. We thank you for the opportunity to serve You, as we are involved in missions. Open our ears, eyes, and heart so that we might serve You more effectively wherever we are. May we be Your church in the world, filled with the power of Your presence. Through Christ, our Living Lord, we pray. Amen.

Father, we thank You for the great good news of Jesus Christ our redeeming Lord. Give us the courage and the boldness to share this good news with all people. We thank You, Lord, for loving us even when we are unlovable. Guide us to share Your joy with others. Through Christ our Lord we pray. Amen.

Gracious God, I marvel at your patience. Sometimes as ministers we become impatient with your church, with ourselves, and with each other. We sometimes wonder how you can be so patient with the church when it is so far from being what You had established it to be. We thank You for Your patience. Give to us, O God, a vision, a dream, of what we can be as Your people, and let us respond to that dream. Through Christ the greatest visionary of all we pray. Amen.

Eternal Father, we are conscious how far we really are from being what You would have us be as Church. Yet we know that You continue to use us as flawed as we are. And we thank You for Your love. May Your love flow through us in a greater way into the world. May we make Your goodness so attractive that all persons will be drawn to You. Through the one who loved us and gave his life for us, we pray. Amen.

O God of Love, we thank You for the church, the church for which Christ gave his life, the church through which he continues to carry on his ministry, and the church that he loved and continues to love. Open us, O Father, to being church more effectively in the world and loving it more. Through Christ who laid down his life for his church. Amen.

O Pioneering God, we have to confess that sometimes we have been content simply to be at church and have not realized that we have been called to be Church. Awaken us, as your ministers, to the task You have given us. May we, for the joy that we have received in Christ, go forth to share this love with others. For we pray it in the strong name of Christ our Lord. Amen.

O God of grace, we thank You for the wonder of Your love that we have experienced in Jesus Christ. We thank You for Your love that reaches beyond our understanding and for the gift of grace which redeems us and makes us whole. Teach us, O God, how to love You more fully and how to serve You more faithfully, as we follow Jesus Christ, our Lord, in whose name we pray. Amen.

O Father make us love You more and want to serve You faithfully as you have faithfully loved us. Amen

5.

OFFERTORY PRAYERS

The brief offertory prayer should express our gratitude for all God's blessings and denote our commitment to sharing our tithes, offerings, and all our gifts in appreciation for God's unending, gracious love and forgiveness.

Gracious God, we offer to You today our tithes and offerings. May they be used to advance Your Kingdom. Through Christ, who gave his all that Your kingdom might come. Amen.

O God of Love, we bring to You our gifts of love and thanksgiving for Your divine grace and love to us. Bless the giver and the gift as we dedicate ourselves to You. Amen.

Giver of all perfect gifts, we bring our gifts to You this day to express our thanksgiving for Your redemption and everlasting love. May our devotion to You grow as we give back to You in this hour. Amen.

Having been blessed beyond our understanding, O God, we offer now to You a small token of our love for You through the tithes and offerings we bring this day. Amen.

Remembering this day, Our Father, the sacrificial death of Your son on the cross, we humbly bring our offering to You. Help us to learn how to give sacrificially as You revealed to us through Your Son's sacrificial death. Amen.

We dedicate these gifts to You today, O Lord. May they be used through our church to honor and glorify Your name. Amen.

We know we can never match Your matchless love, Our Father. Nevertheless, we bring our offerings this day as a token of our devotion and love for You. May they be used to bless Your name and serve Your holy ministry. Amen.

Loving God, we open our hands and hearts now to express our love for You through the offerings we bring. May they be used to show the love and salvation we have experienced through Christ, our Lord. Amen.

O God, we know we can never fully comprehend the depth of Your love we have seen expressed through Your Son, Jesus Christ, yet we seek in these moments to offer these tithes and gifts as a sign of our acknowledgement of that love. May our understanding of Your love grow with the passing of each day. Amen.

O Loving God, we offer our gifts to You this day not out of fear or obligation but out of love and devotion. May they be acceptable in Your sight. Amen.

May the offering we bring this day be acceptable and pleasing to You, O God. We offer these gifts as an expression of our genuine love and devotion to You. Amen.

Eternal God, we acknowledge that each of us has been given grace according to the measure of Christ's gift, so may our gifts reflect the measure of our love for our Lord and our desire to serve Him. Amen.

Loving God, may our tithes and offerings this day help equip us for ministry and in the building up the body of Christ in the world. Unite us in the work of ministry that all we do will enable us to grow in the faith and advance Your Kingdom's work here and around the world. Amen.

Bless the giver and the gifts this day, O Lord. May they be used to advance the spreading of the Gospel of Christ in our community and wherever the witness is needed. Amen.

Divine Father, we know that we have not earned Your love, but You have graciously given it to us out of Your love and grace. May we in turn seek to give our gifts now as an expression of our thankfulness for such love and grace. We bow before You now with gracious hearts. Amen.

Merciful Lord, the giver of every good and perfect gift, grant us the wisdom to use these gifts to further Your Kingdom's work and advance the gospel into the lives of all persons. Amen.

Almighty God, You have prospered us with Your bounty. Enable us to respond with loving kindness and dedicated service with our offerings and faithful witness. Amen.

O God, Who has blessed us with abundance, increase our spirit of thankfulness and desire to share with those whose needs are so great and who have not heard the Good News of the Gospel story. Teach us how to be more willing to give than to receive and consecrate our hearts to Your service. Through Christ, our Lord, we pray. Amen.

"Thine, O Lord, is the greatness, and the power, and the glory, and the victory, and the majesty; for all that is in the heaven and in the earth is thine; thine is the kingdom, O Lord, and Thou art exalted as head above all. Amen." (1Chronicles 29: 11)

6.

BENEDICTIONS

The benediction directs the worshipper's attention to following God's guidance in one's daily life and applying the lessons one sensed in worship that day and leaving with an awareness of God's abiding presence.

May you sense God beside you to comfort you. God behind you to encourage you. God beneath you to support you. God before you to guide you. God above you to sharpen your vision. And most of all God within you to assure you of divine grace and love. Amen.

Depart with God the Father, who is God for us; with Jesus, God the Son, alongside us; with the Holy Spirit, God within us. Amen.

Leave today with the sense of Christ with you, Christ in you, Christ on your side, Christ above you, Christ below you, and Christ before you to guide your way. Amen.

"The Lord bless you and keep you; the Lord make his face to shine upon you and be gracious to you; the Lord lift up his countenance upon you and give you peace" (Numbers 6:24-26).

May Christ be in your heart, in your seeing, in your hearing, in your speaking, and in your living today and in the days to come. Amen.

Loving God, may we leave this place armed with your presence to sustain us and guide us, to fortify us and equip us, to comfort and challenge us today and in the days ahead. Amen.

Now may God fill your heart with joy, your mind with assurance and your heart with love today and all through the days ahead. Amen.

May the love and grace of God the Father, Son and Holy Spirit be in your seeing, your hearing, your speaking, your touching, and in all your living both today and in the days to come. Amen

Leave now with the sense of God's presence before you to guide you, behind you to shield you from harm, below you to strengthen you, above you to enliven you, and within you to direct your spiritual path. Amen.

Leave this place with thankfulness, the assurance of God's love, God's peace to comfort you, and God's grace to sustain you. Amen.

As the Wise Men came seeking the Christ child and fell down to worship him, may we continue to seek his presence and worship him in our daily living as we leave this place. Amen.

Leave now with the joy of the angels' message; the quest of the Wise Men to search for the Christ Child; the shepherds surprise at the manger and the desire always to make room for the Christ whose birth we celebrate. Amen.

Eternal God, give us the assurance that You are with us in our sleeping, working, recreation, conversation, and all our living this day and every day. Amen.

As we leave this sacred place, may the music of Your Spirit fill our lives so that the melody of Your Presence will guide, sustain, fortify, and challenge all our living this week. Amen.

As our Special Friend, who has borne our burdens, sorrows, pain, and sins, strengthen us as we leave this sacred place with the assurance of Your sustaining friendship, and presence. No matter what we face in the days ahead, whether it is joy or sorrow, hopes or fears, good or bad, life or death, may Your abiding companionship sustain us. Amen.

May the love of God the Father, the mercy of the Holy Spirit and the redeeming grace of Jesus Christ be with you this day and in the days to come. Amen.

May the God of eternal love and new beginnings inspire you to new opportunities for service and witness in the days ahead. Amen.

May God beneath you sustain you as you leave today. May God above you refresh you with determination to serve better. May God behind you support you during difficult times. May God before you guide your way. May God within inspire you each step of the way. Amen.

May God bless and keep you. May his face shine upon you and be gracious to you. Amen.

May the peace of Christ go with you. May the Spirit guide you through the wildernesses where you may travel. May the Father protect you through the storms you encounter. May the wonder of the love of God the Father, Son and Spirit bring you home rejoicing. Amen.

Leave today with Christ as your light. Leave today with the Spirit as your shield. Leave today with the Father as your Rock of salvation. Amen.

Depart today with the assurance of Christ beside you; Christ above you; Christ beneath you; Christ behind you; Christ ahead of you; Christ within you. Amen.

May Christ illumine and guide you. May Christ strengthen and undergird you. May Christ encourage and enliven you. May Christ love and bless you now and in the days ahead. Amen.

May the Creator God, the Wounded Savior, and the Strengthening Spirit give you creative insight, sacrificial service and courageous living in the days that lie before you. Amen.

The grace of our Lord Jesus Christ, and the love of God, the Father, and the communion of the Holy Spirit, be with you all. Amen.

Grace, mercy, and peace from God the Father, Son, and Holy Spirit, be with you now and forever more. Amen.

Go forth today with the assurance of Almighty God's presence with you, and your mind enlightened by the renewed knowledge of Christ's way, and your heart warmed by the gracious mercy of the Holy Spirit. Amen.

"Peace be to the whole community, and love with faith, from God the Father and the Lord Jesus Christ. Grace be with all who have undying love for our Lord Jesus Christ." (Ephesians 6:23-24)

Easter

May the Risen Christ stand beside you to strengthen you; behind you to guard you from falling; before you to guide you; above you to give you vision; below you to comfort you, and within you to inspire you. Amen

7.

AFFIRMATIONS OF FAITH AND LITANIES

Affirmations of Faith or Litanies summon the worshipper to express with others in the congregation assurances of one's beliefs or confessions of one's sins and a quest for a stronger faith. They are a means of involving the congregation directly in the spoken dimension of the worship service.

EASTER AFFIRMATION OF FAITH (IN UNISON)

This is the good news which we have received, in which we stand, and by which we are saved,

that Christ died for our sins according to the Scriptures, that He was buried,

that He was raised on the third day, and that He appeared, first to Mary, then to Peter, and to the Twelve, and then to many faithful witnesses. We believe that Jesus is the Christ, the Son of the living God.

Jesus Christ is the first and the last, the beginning and the end.

He is our Lord and our God. Amen.

BAPTISMAL AFFIRMATION

We celebrate the baptism today of ----- and ----.

We acknowledge their desire to follow Christ as Lord of their lives.

We know they will need guidance and support in their Christian journey.

We will support them with our prayers, encouragement, and love with God's help.

LITANIES

A Litany For The New Year

Leader: Last year is behind us and we look now to the year before us.

People: We acknowledge sins, mistakes, uncompleted tasks, and hopes not realized.

Leader: Forgive us for past undoing's and give us faith and courage to move forward with confidence in the new year before us.

People: We affirm our need for the presence and guidance of Christ as we journey into the new year.

Leader: May we be alert to the needs around us and our responsibility to reach out to help the needy, ill, troubled, and any who have genuine calamities.

People: Help us to be the instruments in Christ's service for these people.

Unison: Give us guidance and strength to go into this new year with the desire to be Christlike in our personal lives and in our relationship with others.

A Litany Of Good Will

Leader: The Church declares boldly that God is the Creator of all persons.

People: We thank God for our Creator's divine love and grace.

Leader: We acknowledge, however, that racism has a long history in our world.

People: Forgive us, O God, when we have allowed prejudice to determine our relationship with other persons.

Leader: May Jesus Christ help us to break down all racial barriers and enable us to love all persons as Christ accepts and loves us.

People: May we be bridge-builders to witness to Christ's transcending love that crosses all barriers, persons, sexes, and races.

Unison: As God welcomes all persons with divine love, grant that we will work for racial harmony and good will toward all persons. Amen.

Affirmation Of Faith

Minister: Jesus said to His disciples, "My meat is to do the will of Him that sent me, and to finish his work". (John 4:34)

People: We believe that whoever does the will of God is vitally related to Jesus Christ. (Mark 3:35)

Minister: Jesus prayed in Gethsemane, "If it be possible, let this cup pass from me: nevertheless, not as I will, but as Thou wilt". (Matthew 26:39)

People: We believe that we must pray earnestly and sincerely. "Thy kingdom come. Thy will be done, as in Heaven, so in earth". (Matthew 6:10)

Unison: We believe that Christianity is more than saying that Jesus Christ is Lord. We must, also, do the will of the Father. (Matthew 7:21)

Minister: We believe that Jesus Christ is the first and the last, the Living One, who was dead but is now alive for timeless ages. (Revelations 1:17, 18)

People: We believe that if a person desires to be a Christian, he or she must give up all rights to oneself, carry one's cross every day, and keep close behind Christ. (Luke 2:23)

Minister: We believe that if one is in Christ, he and she becomes a new person – the past is finished and gone, and life has become fresh and new. (2 Corinthians 5:17)

Unison: We believe that Christians are imperfect, that they have not "arrived" spiritually. We also believe that Christians must keep going on, grasping ever more firmly that purpose for which Christ grasped them. (Philippians 3:12)

An Affirmation Of Faith

Minister: "When the Word goes forth, it gives light and understanding to the simple." (Psalm 119:130)

People: "For not by the will of anyone was prophecy at any time, but persons being borne by the Holy Spirit from God." (2 Peter 1:21)

Minister: "In many and various ways God spoke of old to our fathers by the prophets, but in these last days God has spoken to us by a Son." (Hebrews 1:1)

People: "In the beginning was the Word, and the Word was with God and the Word was God." (John 1:1)

Minister: "And the Word became flesh and dwelt among us, full of grace and truth; we have beheld his glory, glory as of the only Son from the Father." (John 1:14)

People: "You search the scriptures, because you think in them to have eternal life, and these are they which bear witness concerning me." (John 24:27)

Minister: "Their eyes were opened, and they recognized this: and he vanished from their sight. And they said to one another, Did not our hearts burn within us as he was speaking to us along the way, and he opened to us the scriptures?" (John 24:31-32)

Unison: "Many other signs did Jesus in the presence of his disciples which are not written in this book; but these have been written in order that you might trust that Jesus is the Christ, the

Son of God, and that trusting you might have life in his name."
(John 20:30-31)

An Affirmation Of Praise

From "Songs of Thanksgiving"
In the Dead Sea Scrolls
(In addition to the many Psalms expressing thankfulness,
found in our Bibles, we have further similar devotional meditations
from the Jews of the Dead Sea community, on scrolls buried before
the time of Christ and recently found.)

Minister: I thank thee, O Lord, because thou hast put my soul
in the bundle of life;
People: Thou hast brought me up to an eternal height, and I
walk in an unsearchable plain. I know that there is hope for one
whom thou hast formed from the dust for an eternal company.
Minister: For God thunders with the noise of his might.
People: I thank thee, O Lord, because thou hast sustained me
with thy strength, and hast shed abroad thy Holy Spirit in me.
Minister: I thank thee, O Lord, because thou hast made me
wise in thy truth and in the wondrous mysteries hast given me
knowledge.
People: I thank thee, O Lord, because thou hast done wondrously
with dust, with a thing formed of clay thou hast done powerfully.
Unison: I will praise thy name among those who fear thee, with
songs of thanksgiving and prayer.

Affirmation Of Faith

Minister: Happy are those who know they are spiritually poor:
the Kingdom of Heaven belongs to them.
People: Happy are those who mourn: God will comfort them.

Minister: Happy are the meek: They will receive what God has promised.

People: Happy are those whose greatest desire is to do what God requires: God will satisfy them fully.

Minister: Happy are those who show mercy to others: God will show mercy to them.

People: Happy are the pure in heart: they will see God.

Minister: Happy are those who work for peace among all people: God will call them his sons.

People: Happy are those who suffer persecution because they do what God requires: the Kingdom of heaven belongs to them!

Unison: Happy are you when persons insult you and mistreat you and tell all kinds of evil lies against you because you are my followers. Rejoice and be glad because a great reward is kept for you in heaven. This is how men mistreated the prophets who lived before you.

Matthew 5:1-11 (Good News for Modern Man)

Affirmation Of Faith

Leader: We believe in God, the Eternal Spirit, Father of our Lord Jesus Christ and our Father, the Creator of our world.

People: God calls the worlds into existence being Creator and in his own image and sets before humanity the ways of life and death. God seeks in holy love to save all people from sinlessness and sin.

Leader: He judges humanity and nations by his righteousness and declares his will through prophets and apostles.

People: In Jesus Christ, the son of Nazareth, our crucified and risen Lord, God has come to us and shared our common lot, conquering sin and death and reconciling the world to himself.

Leader: He beacons upon me his Holy Spirit, creating and renewing the Church of Jesus Christ, binding in covenant faithful people of all ages.

People: He calls us into his Church to accept the call and joy of discipleship to be his servants in the service of all persons, to proclaim the gospel to all the world and to resist the powers of evil, to adhere in Christ to baptism and sit at his table, to join him in this passion and victory.

Together: He promises to all who trust him forgiveness of sins and fullness of grace, courage in the struggle for justice and peace, his presence in trial and rejoicing, and eternal life in his kingdom which has no end. Blessing and honor, glory, and power be unto his children. Amen.

The Celebration Of Childhood

Pastor: What are you holding in your arms?

Parents: We are holding the mystery of God's ongoing creation. We hold spirit made flesh in the image of God.

Pastor: What are you holding in your mind?

Parents: We are holding the vision of the future and the responsibilities of the present. We are reaffirming the disciplines of parenthood.

Pastor: What are you holding in your dreams?

Parents: We are holding the hope that we might lead this child to a wholesome experience of his (her) own worth before God and others.

Pastor: What are you holding in your hearts?

Parents: We are holding the deepest desire to nurture this child with a kind Christ-like love that will enable her (him) to grow towards God and man.

Pastor: And what do we behold:

Congregation: We behold the joy we have together as God's children to pledge our best prayers and effort to the nurture of these children and their families in the faith of our Lord.

All: May God grant us courage as we all try to grow up as did Jesus: in wisdom and favor with God and man.

Pastor: Pastor offers a Prayer of Dedication

The Litany Of Youth

Minister: O God, who through the Spirit in the young carpenter of Nazareth changed the face of the world and in every age calls the fresh vigor of new life to thy service, we pray thee for the youth of our generation.

People: What the elders by their sin have put out of order, strengthen the new generation with wisdom to cure and with righteousness to establish.

Minister: Guard the character of our youth and preserve their integrity against the day of thy call to service.   Now in the springtime of their years may they not strip blooms from their trees to make transient garlands of pleasure, only to find when autumn comes that there is no growth.

People: From flippancy and cynicisms, from deadening unbelief and purposeless living, from vulgar tastes and sensual deeds, Good Lord, deliver them.

Minister: From mistaking license for liberty, from surrender to the tyranny of undisciplined desires, from the slavery of habits which, free to begin, they are not free to stop, Good Lord, deliver them.

People: We praise thee for the zest and radiance of youth and for the untamed hopes with which the young continually refresh the earth, and since old customs, grown too old, corrupt the world, use thou in our time their undimmed eyes to see and their undiscouraged vigor to achieve thy will.

Unison: Enlist their unbroken strength in service; temper their releases into moral courage; out of their youthful spirit of daring bring the maturity of independent minds and venturesome endeavors; and so lead them from youth to age that, dishonored and unashamed, they may transmit to their children a better world than ours.

Adapted from a Litany by Harry Emerson Fosdick, A Book of Public Prayers, (New York: Harper Brothers, 1959)

The Litany Of Growth

Minister: O God, who has called us to newness of life and openness of spirit, grant that our minds and hearts may ever be open to the continuous guidance of thy spirit.

People: Free us from the fear of adventuresome living and the constant desire for the certain, secure, safe, and familiar.

Minister: In our short journey of life, keep us receptive to the one who said: "I am come that they may have life, and that they may have it more abundantly." (John 10:10)

People: O God, who has founded thy church to be the pillar and support of the truth; grant that all who claim membership therein may really love and follow truth.

Minister: Save us from slipshod or dishonest thinking. Forbid that we should turn away from any question because we do not know, or because we fear to give, the answer. May we never regard as enemies those who reach conclusions which differ from our own.

People: In our quest for Christian maturity, grant that the master Teacher may continue to instruct us so that we might grow physically, intellectually, aesthetically, morally, and spiritually.

Minister: May our lives reflect that we are alive to the great gift of life itself. May we be ever growing, sensitive and responsive, attuned with thy power which is the source of life itself.

Unison: Strengthen us to read and think and work with courage and humility, confident that as we seek to grow in the truth, we shall not lack the guidance of thy spirit.

A Litany For Advancing Years

Minister: O God, whose years are throughout all generations, we acknowledge that you abide though all else passes away.

People: We thank you for the gift of our days and the knowledge of your companionship in our past and the assurance of your love and friendship in the future.

Minister: Teach us to see that life itself is a gift, to enjoy and cherish while we have it. Grant that we may sense that the Giver is greater still and that life in God never dies.

People: Help us to make the noblest use of mind and body in our advancing years, according to our strength and apportion for our work. As you have pardoned our transgressions, sift the ingathering of our memory, that evil may grow dim and good may shine forth clearly.

Minister: Keep us from narrow pride in outgrown ways, blind eyes that will not see the good of change, and impatient judgements of the methods and experiments of others.

People: Grant us new ties of friendship, new opportunities of service, joy in the growth and happiness of children, sympathy with those who bear the burdens of the world, clear thoughts and quiet faith.

Minister: Take from us, O Lord, all despair of the world, all regret of vanished days, fill every day with deepest living and give us a forward look a joyous faith and continuous sense of the wonder of the mystery of life.

People: Amid the shadows of evening, grant us the vision of your glorious morning, O God. May the radiance of your presence enable us to rejoice to know that darkness and light are both alike to you. Abide with us, O Lord, that in fellowship with you, we may share in the life everlasting.

A Litany Of Faith

Minister: We praise thee, O God, for the rich and productive spiritual heritage which has been ours as Baptists. We acknowledge with gratitude the devotion and sacrifices which have brought us to this hour in our Christian pilgrimage.

People: O Lord, make us thankful.

Minister: We thank thee for the poets, artists, musicians, teachers, ministers, writers, and all seers who have enlarged our vision to perceive eternal truth and love. For those who have labored quietly or illustriously.

People: O Lord, make us grateful.

Minister: Enable us, O Lord to accept the legacy which has come to us from the past with thanksgiving and rededicate ourselves to the redemptive mission of the church in the world today.

People: Strengthen us for this task, O Lord.

Minister: Aware, O Lord, of the great host of witnesses compassed about us and sensitive to the guidance of Christ who is head of the church, challenge us to a vital commitment to Thee.

People: Strengthen our vow of commitment, O Lord, that we might serve thee with our prayers, presence, gifts, and service.

Minister: May the Eternal Spirit of Christ lift our hearts above the harsh confusions of our time, above its apathy and chaos, and refresh our souls with courage, peace, joy, and love.

People: We beseech Thee to hear us, O Lord.

Minister: O God, who has called us to newness of life and openness of spirit, grant that our minds and hearts may be open to the Master Teacher so that we might continue to grow physically, intellectually, aesthetically, morally, and spiritually.

People: Lord, have mercy upon us and incline our hearts to thy creativity.

Minister: Free us from the fear of adventuresome living and the constant desire for the certain, secure, safe, and familiar.

People: Hear our prayer, O Lord.

Union: O God of grace, grant us an openness of mind and heart to sense thy presence at work in the words, sounds and colors of our age. Give us wisdom, give us courage that we might seek to be agents of reconciliation in the world. Amen.

The Love Litany

Minister: I'm giving you a new rule. This is it. Love each other. That's right, just like I've loved you, you love one another.

Congregation: If you do this, everyone will know you're my disciples. If you love one another, if you love one another.

Minister: Don't get hung up in bitterness or wrath or anger or feuding or saying hateful things about people. Put this aside.

Congregation: And be kind to one another. Be tenderhearted. Forgive one another, just as God for Christ's sake has forgiven you. And love one another.

Minister: With love, you can offer love, with love, you are kind. Love has no envy, love puts no one above one's brother or sister.

Congregation: Love does not like hate, nor does it love only "its own kind." Christian love thinks no evil and rejoices in truth.

Minister: Love makes it unable to hear tough things, makes one able to believe, have hope, and to endure.

Congregation: Love never fails.

Minister: Prophecies might fail, tongues may stop, and knowledge could vanish.

Congregation: But love never fails.

Minister: So now you have faith, hope, and love. These three. But the greatest is love.

Congregation: And the greatest love is God's, for he gave his Son's life for you. Will you give your life for your brother and sister?

Minister: Will you, with your affluence, with you world's goals, see your brother or sister in need, and will you strife your compassion for them? Will you love God and watch your brother or sister suffer?

Congregation: No! Love is not merely words. Love is action, love is deeds done in God's name.

Minister: Christian Friends. let us love one another. For love is of God. And everyone that loves other persons knows God. For God is love.

A Litany Of The Christ

Minister: Jesus said, "You have heard that it was said to persons of old, "You shall not kill; and whoever kills shall be liable to judgement."

People: "But I say to you that everyone who is angry with his brother or sister shall be liable to judgement: whoever insults his brother or sister shall be liable to the council, and whoever says, "you fool!" shall be liable to the hell of fire."

Minister: Jesus said, "Again you have heard that it was said to the persons of old, "you shall not swear falsely, but shall perform to the Lord what you have sworn."

People: "But I say to you, Do not swear at all, either by heaven, for it is the throne of God, or by the earth, for it is his footstool, or by Jerusalem, for it is the city of the great King."

Minister: Jesus said, "you have heard that is was said, "An eye for an eye and a tooth for a tooth."

People: "But I say to you, Do not resist one who is evil. But if anyone strikes you on the right cheek, turn to him or her the other also; and if anyone would sue you and take your coat, let that person have your cloak as well; and if anyone forces you to one mile, go with them two miles."

Minister: Jesus said, "You have heard that it was said, 'You shall love your neighbor and hate your enemy."

People: "But I say to you, Love your enemies and pray for those who persecute you, so that you may be sons of your Father who is in heaven."

Unison: But perhaps Jesus' hardest words were, "You, therefore, must be perfect, as your heavenly Father is perfect." O Lord, may we so strive to be.

   From The Sermon On The Mount

A Prayer: Remembering Christ's Suffering

Minister: O Thou whose eternal love for our weak and struggling race was most perfectly shown forth in the blessed life and death of Jesus Christ, our Lord, enable me now so to meditate upon my Lord's passion that, having fellowship with Him in His sorrow, I may also learn the secret of His strength and peace.

People: I remember Gethsemane:
               I remember how Judas betrayed Him:
               I remember how Peter denied Him:
               I remember how they all forsook Him and fled:

Minister: I remember the scourging:
               I remember the crown of thorns:
               I remember how they spat upon Him:
               I remember how they smote Him on the head
               with a reed:

People: I remember His pierced hands and feet:
               I remember His agony on the Cross:
               I remember His thirst:

> I remember how He cried, My God, my God,
> why hast Thou forsaken me?

Minister: We may not know, we cannot tell,
> what pains He had to bear.
> But we believe it was for us.
> He hung and suffered there.

Unison: Grant, O most gracious God, that I, who now kneel before Thee, may be embraced in the great company of those to whom life and salvation have come through the Cross of Christ. Let the redeeming power that has flowed from His suffering through so many generations flow now into my soul. Here let me find forgiveness of sin. Here let me learn to share with Christ the burden of the suffering of the world. Amen.

John Baillie, *A Diary of Private Prayer* (New York: Charles Scribner's Sons, 1949), p. 71

A Confession Of Sin

Minister: We are many and we are varied. Is there reason to believe that we can somehow break down the barriers of communication between us? Can we overcome the appalling silence that exists when we meet and are unable to hear each other's needs?

People: If our hope to find meaning for our lives is not a hope, then we can learn to hear each other as we come to worship God.

Unison: We confess that at times we have not listened and acknowledged when others have pains and special needs. We confess our failures and long for guidance from Christ's hand

Minister: Father, help us to know our own feelings, but more importantly help us to understand the feelings of those around us. Teach us to be aware. Teach us to communicate. Give us the courage to break the silence with which the world is encountering and lead us to understanding. Give us wisdom.

Unison: Father, help us to discover the change Your Spirit can make within us when we know the forgiveness of our sins and the capacity for goodness You can make within us. Thank you for the fulfillment for the new direction we feel. Lead us to understanding. Give us wisdom. Amen.

A Prayer For Forgiveness

Minister: O Father in heaven, who didst fashion my limbs to serve thee and my soul to follow hard after thee, with sorrow and contrition of heart, I acknowledge before thee the faults and failures of the day that is now past.

People: Too long, O Father, have I tried thy patience; too often have I betrayed the sacred trust thou hast given me to keep; yet thou art still willing that I should come to thee in lowliness of heart, as now I do, beseeching thee to drown my transgressions in the sea of thine own infinite love.

Minister: My failure to be true even to my own accepted standards:

My self-deception in face of temptation:
My choosing of the worse when I know the **better:**
O Lord, forgive.

People: My failure to apply to myself the standards of conduct I demand of others:

Minister: My blindness to the suffering of others and my slowness to be taught by my own:

People: My complacency towards wrongs that do not touch my own case and my over-sensitiveness to those that do:

Minister: My slowness to see the good in my fellows and to see the evil in myself:

Unison: My hardness of heart towards my neighbors' faults and my readiness to make allowance for my own:

My unwillingness to believe that thou hast called me to a small work and my brother to a greater one:

O Lord, forgive.

John Baillie, *A Diary of Private Prayer*, page 15.

A Covenant Of Service

Minister: "And these were his gifts: some to be apostles, some prophets, some evangelists, some pastors and some teachers, to equip God's people for work in his service, to the building up of the body of Christ." Ephesians 4:11-12.

People: "I am no prophet, nor a prophet's son; but I am a herdsman, and a dresser of sycamore trees, and the lord took me from following the flock, and the Lord said to me, 'Go, prophesy to my people Israel." Amos 7:14-15.

Minister: "But you are a chosen race, a royal priesthood, a holy nation. God's own people, that you may declare the wonderful deeds of him who called you out of darkness into his marvelous light." 1 Peter 2:9.

People: "Maintain good conduct among the Gentiles, so that in case they speak against you as wrong doers, they may see your good deeds and glorify God." 1 Peter 2:12.

Minister: "You have been born anew, not of perishable seed but of imperishable, through the living and abiding word of God." 1 Peter 1: 23.

People: "Know, therefore, that the Lord your God is God, the faithful God who keeps covenant and steadfast love with those who love him and keep his commandments." Deuteronomy 7: 9.

Minister: "Christ loved the Church and gave himself up for her, that he might sanctify her, having cleansed her by the washing of water with the word." Ephesians 5:25.

People: "That the Church might be presented before him in splendor, without spot or wrinkle or any such things, that she might be holy and without blemish." Ephesians 5:26-27.

Minister: "There are varieties of gifts, but the same Spirit. There are varieties of service, but the same Lord." 1 Corinthians 12:5-6.

Unison: "There are many forms of work, but all of them, in all persons, are the work of the same God. In each of us the Spirit is manifested in one particular way, for some useful purpose." 1 Corinthians 12:6-8.

A Litany Of Rejoicing

Minister: Rejoice and hear the voice of God as spoken to Moses: "I AM WHO I AM. Say this to the people of Israel, 'I AM has sent me to you.'"(Exodus 3: 14)

People: Let us respond and hear the voice of God: "The Lord, the God of your fathers, the God of Abraham, the God of Isaac, and the God of Jacob, has sent me to you: this is my name forever, and thus I am to be remembered throughout all generations."(Exodus 3:15)

Minister: Let us also listen to the words of the psalmist, who prayed, "And those who know they name put their trust in thee, for thou, O Lord, hast not forsaken those who seek thee. (Psalm 9:10).

People: Isaiah envisioned the coming of the One whose "name will be called 'Wonderful Counselor, Mighty God, Everlasting Father, Prince of Peace'." (Isaiah 9:6)

Minister: The angel prophesied of his coming: "And you shall call his name Jesus, for he will save his peopled from their sins. And his name shall be called Emmanuel, which means, 'God with us'." (Matthew 1:21, 23).

People: And with us he was, and still is, and evermore shall be! "I made known to them thy name, and I will make it known, that the love with which thou hast loved me may be in them, and I in them." (John 17:26).

Unison: And let us rejoice and give thanks "that at the name of Jesus every knee should bow, in heaven and on earth and under the earth, and every tongue confess that Jesus Christ is Lord, to the glory of God the Father." (Philippians 2:10-11).

A Confessional Prayer For Freedom

Minister: Dear God, to you who has created us for freedom, consistently delivered your people out of captivity, and through the gift of your Son, provided for the redemptive freedom of all, we confess our sins and pray for liberty.

People: Frequently, we have taken for granted the contributions of those who risked their lives, fortunes, and honor for the establishment of freedom and overlooked the sacrifices of those who have given of themselves for the maintenance of freedom. Lord, forgive us.

Minister: While we enjoy the benefits of both civil and religious freedoms and are willing to strengthen the guarantees of those for ourselves, we tend to take lightly, ignore, or even infringe upon the liberties of others. Lord, forgive us.

Peoples: Lifestyles which spend too much, eat too much, and care too little are directly related to the tragedies of our contemporaries who are enslaved in the grinding cycle of poverty or in servitude to the gnawing hunger pains of their stomachs. Lord, forgive us.

Minister: Failure to assume the duties of Christian citizenship have caused us to jeopardize the viability of an open political system and to weaken the foundations of freedom. Lord, forgive us. With your help Lord, we will do better and let freedom ring. Amen

A Prayer For Christian Love

Minister: Father, kindle the spark of love within us to a consuming flame that destroys all barriers.

People: Teach us the meaning of Christian love. May in all our loving be contained the essential ingredient of each of ourselves. In our attempts to love, may we determine that "the only real gift is a portion of myself." (Emerson)

Minister: Father, as we love, guide us to understand the complexities of love, Give us courage – that we fail not anyone nor you.

People: Help us to understand that people are real.
Help us to understand that faces have names.
Help us to understand that bodies are persons.
Help us to understand that love is more than sex.
Help us to understand that people have feelings.
Help us to understand that love requires responsibility.

Minister: Free us, Father, from false deceptions about love. Give us strength to find a self-giving love and a sense of the sacredness of sexuality.

People: Lord, forgive us for being willing to remain in brokenness when your spirit has called us to wholeness and completeness. Breathe the life-giving power of your spirit into our lives and penetrate the depths of our spirits with the note of your love.

Unison: Father, in you we know who we are and in submission to you we understand our fellow man and woman and our responsibility to them. We put our trust in the power of Jesus Christ to make us whole. We trust in his strength to give us the courage to undertake a new task, to begin a new dream, to live a new life.

A Prayer During Times Of Difficulty

Minister: Our Father, in spite of the present difficulty, you are still in heaven and the world is still ordered. May my response hallow your name.

People: The coming of your kingdom is more important than my own difficulty – so may I not hinder its coming by my worry.

Minister: Cause this time to be an opening up to your will for earth which I can see as clearly as if I were in heaven.

People: I must recognize that you still provide the necessities of life: I have bread enough.

Minister: May this difficulty help me to realize how important it is to secure your forgiveness and to forgive those who have sinned against me.

People: And may this not be an occasion for temptation to lose faith or respond as a pagan.

Minister: Deliver me from any evil response or action in this difficulty.

Unison: The overriding and all-important fact of life is that to you belongs the kingdom and the power and the glory forever, and this even is caught up in that fact.   Amen

A Prayer Of Confession

Minister: "Have mercy upon us, O God, according to your lovingkindness;"

People: "According to the multitude of your tender mercies blot out our transgressions."

Minister: "Wash us thoroughly from our iniquities, and cleanse us from our sins."

People: "For we acknowledge our transgressions, and our sin is ever before us."

Minister: "Purge us, and we shall be clean;"

People: "Wash us and we shall be whiter than snow."

Minister: "Create in us clean hearts, O God;"

People: "And renew a right spirit within us."

Unison: "Cast us not away from your presence and take not your Holy Spirit from us. Amen"

    Psalm 51

A Litany Of Work

Minister: Then God said, "Let us make man in our image, after our likeness; and let them have dominion over the fish of the sea, and over the birds of the air, and over all the earth, and over every creeping thing that creeps upon the earth." (Genesis 1:26)

People: "So God created man in his own image, in the image of God he created him; male and female he created them." (Genesis 1:27)

Minister: "The Lord took the man and put him in the garden of Eden to till it and keep it." (Genesis 2:15)

People: "Remember the sabbath day, to keep it holy. Six days you shall labor and do all your work; but the seventh day is a sabbath to the Lord your God; in it you shall not do any work…". (Exodus 20:8-10)

Minister: "Blessed is everyone who fears the Lord, who walks in his ways! You shall eat the fruit of the labor of your hands; you shall be happy, and it shall be well with you." (Psalm 128:1-2)

People: "But we exhort you, brethren…to aspire to live quietly, to mind your own affairs, and to work with your hands, as we charged you; so that you may command the respect of an outsider and be dependent on nobody." (1 Thessalonians 4:10-12)

Minister: "But Jesus answered them, 'My Father is working still, and I am working.'" (John 5:17)

Unison: "We must work the works of him who sent me, while it is day; night comes, when no one can work." (John 9:4)

A Litany On Speaking

Minister: "The words of a man's mouth are deep waters; the fountain of wisdom is a gushing stream." Proverbs 18:4

People: "Who shall dwell on the holy hill? He who walks blamelessly, and does what is right, and speaks truth from his heart; who does not slander with his tongue." Psalm 15:1-3

Minister: "The words of a wise man's mouth win him favor, but the lips of a fool consume him." Ecclesiastes 10:12

People: "A lying tongue hates its victims, and a flattering mouth works ruin." Proverbs 26:28

Minister: "Your tongue is like a sharp razor. You love evil more than good and lying more than speaking the truth." Psalm 52:2-3

People: "Death and life are in the power of the tongue, and those who love it will eat its fruits." Proverbs 18:21

Minister: "A word fitly spoken is like apples of gold in a setting of silver." Proverbs 25:11

People: "Let no one despise your youth but set the believers an example in speech and conduct, in love, in faith, in purity." 1 Timothy 4:12

Minister: "I tell you, on the day of judgment, men will render account for every careless word they utter; for by your words you will be justified, and by your words you will be condemned." Matthew 12:36-37

Unison: "And whatever you do, in word or deed, do everything in the name of the Lord Jesus, giving thanks to God the Father through him." Colossians 3:17

A Prayer For The Church

Minister: O God, we pray for thy church, which is set today amid the perplexities of a changing order, face to face with a great new task.

People: We remember with love the nurture she gave to our spiritual life in its infancy, the task she set for our growing strength, the influence of the devoted hearts she gathers, the steadfast power for good she has exerted.

Minister: When we compare her with all human institutions, we rejoice, for there is none like her. But when we judge her by the mind of her Master, we bow in pity and contrition.

People: Oh, baptize her afresh in the life-giving spirit of Jesus! Grant her a new birth, though it be with the travail of repentance and humiliation.

Minister: Bestow upon her a more imperious responsiveness to duty, a swifter compassion with suffering, and an utter loyalty to the will of God. Put upon her lips the ancient gospel of her Lord, Help her to proclaim boldly the coming of the Kingdom of God.

People: Fill her with a prophet's scorn of tyranny and with a Christ-like tenderness for the poor, weak and needy. Bid her cease from seeking her own life, lest she lose it.

Unison: Make her valiant to give up her life to humanity, that, like her crucified Lord, she may mount by the path of thy cross to a higher glory.

Walter Rauschenbusch, *Prayers for the Social Awakening*, (Boston: The Pilgrim Press, 1909), p. 119.

Church Covenant

Minister: United in the faith that Jesus Christ is the Son of God, revealed in history, disclosed in the Scriptures, and experienced in human life, we do solemnly and joyfully make this Covenant together:

People: That we will be faithful in the assembling of ourselves together for worship, be diligent in praying both for ourselves and others; be constant in our reading and studying of the Bible;

Minister: That we will be faithful stewards, as God has prospered us, contributing our financial support for the Church and its ministries, and offering ourselves for God's work in the world;

People: That we will be a servant Church, recognizing the infinite worth of every person and believing that Christ has called us to active involvement in behalf of human brotherhood;

Minister: That we will participate in each other's joys, and endeavor with tenderness and sympathy to bear each other's burdens and sorrows;

People: That we will exercise a Christian care and watchfulness over each other; and that our differences will not separate us but rather increase our understanding and strengthen the bonds of Christian love;

Minister: That we will earnestly endeavor to take seriously the responsibility and privilege of personal Christian growth, diligently seeking to establish and maintain a Christian atmosphere in our homes, and that we will with God's help, so live our lives that we might lead our kindred and acquaintances to know Jesus Christ our Lord;

People: That we will, should we move from this church, unite with another church as soon as possible, where we can carry out the spirit of this covenant;

Union: And that through life, in the midst of evil as well as good, we will seek to live to the glory of Him who has called us out of darkness into His marvelous light.

First Baptist Church Covenant, Bristol, Virginia. Adopted April 28, 1976

A Litany Of Stewardship

Minister: Grant us, Lord, the grace of giving with a spirit large and free, that ourselves and all our living we may offer unto Thee.

People: O Lord, I acknowledge that Christian stewardship is the dedication of all I am and have, under the control of the Spirit of Christ – to the doing of his will, in recognition of his Lordship, in gratitude for his love, in every area of life, and in the serving of his redemptive fellowship.

Minister: I am only one – but still I am one; I cannot do everything, but still, I can do something. And because I cannot do everything, I will not refuse to do something I can do.

People: Unto Thee, O Lord, do we offer the gift of our hands and the loyalty of our hearts.

Minister: To the preaching of the good tidings of salvation.

People: We consecrate our gifts.

Minister: To the teaching Jesus' way of life.

People: We consecrate our gifts.

Minister: To the healing of broken bodies and the soothing of fevered brows.

People: We consecrate our gifts.

Minister: To the leading of every little child to the knowledge and love of Jesus.

People: We consecrate our gifts.

Minister: To the caring of helpless age and relief of all who look to us for help.

People: We consecrate our gifts.

Minister: To the evangelization of the world and spreading the good news of the Kingdom of God.

People: We consecrate our gifts, our efforts, and our lives.

A Litany Of Thanksgiving

Minister: "Let us come before his presence with thanksgiving." Psalms 95:2

People: We give thanks to God for his good news in the midst of the world's bad news.

Minister: "It is good to give thanks unto the Lord, and to sing praises unto His name."

People: Thank God that we can affirm God's eternal "yes" in the midst of the world's "no."

Minister: "Hallelujah! Give thanks to the Eternal! He is good." Psalms 105:1

People: Thanks be to God for his "nevertheless" in the midst of the world's "never."

Minister: "Always give thanks for everything to God the Father." Ephesians 5:20a

People: We give thanks to God in spite of thankless circumstances.

Minister: "He took bread, and gave thanks, and broke it." Luke 22:19

People: Thank God for his mercy which heals our brokenness and sin.

Minister: "The Lord bringeth thee into a good land." Deuteronomy 8:7

Unison: Thanks be to God that we are given the promise of the future for the despair of the present. We give thanks with hope.

A Prayer Of Thanksgiving

Minister: O Almighty Lord God, we lift up our hearts in gratitude to thee for the land of our birth. For the seas that wash our shores, and for this beautiful and fertile land:

People: We thank thee, O God, And praise thy holy name

Minister: For the stirring history of our people, for the achievements of our fathers both at home and overseas, and for all the leaders, heroes, and saints of the past:

People: We thank thee, O God, And praise they holy name

Minister: For the heritage of our common life, for freedom and wise government, for education and the benefits we enjoy through science and invention, through literature and art:

People: We thank thee, O God, And praise they holy name

Minister: For all those who are no fighting crime and social evil, for all who are striving for just laws and better institutions, and for all who are seeking to uphold Christian standards in the press, the cinema, radio, television, the internet, email, and all social media:

People: We thank thee, O God, And praise thy holy name

Minister: For the influence and witness of thy church in this land, for the devoted thought and work of all those in our own denomination who help us to understand and accept responsibilities of citizenship, and for all which, by thy grace, we ourselves have been able to do:

People: We thank thee, O God, And praise thy holy name. Accept this, our sacrifice of thanksgiving, through Jesus Christ our Lord. Amen.

A Declaration Of Faith At Christmas

Minister: I believe in Jesus Christ and in the beauty of the gospel that began in Bethlehem.

People: I believe in him whose spirit glorified a little town, of whose coming only shepherds saw the sign, and for whom the crowded inn could find no room.

Minister: I believe in him whom the kings of the earth ignored. And the proud could never understand, whose welcome came from men of hungry hearts.

People: I believe in him who proclaimed the love of God to be invincible,

Whose cradle was a mother's arms,

Whose home in Nazareth had love for its only wealth,

Who looked at all persons and made them see what his love saw in them.

Who by his love brought sinners back to purity

And lifted human weakness up to meet the strength of God.

Minister: I confess our everlasting need of God, the need of forgiveness for our greed and selfishness. The need of life for empty souls, the need of love for hearts grown, cold.

People: I acknowledge the glory of all that is like Christ, the steadfastness of friends, the blessedness of homes, the beauty of compassion, the miracle of many hearts made kind at Christmas, the courage of those who dare to resist all passion, hate, and war.

Unison: I believe that only by love expressed shall the earth at length be purified. And I acknowledge in Christ a faith that sees beyond the partial fact, a trust in life redeemed that looks beyond our present evil; and I pray that this redemption may begin in us.

A Christmas Prayer

Minister: O Father of all, that we may be prepared for the coming of your Son, the Babe of Bethlehem,

People: Help us to rid our hearts of selfishness, thoughtlessness, and vain pride.

Minister: In a world filled with so much bad news,

People: Help us to receive the "good news" of great joy.

Minister: As Mary, the Mother, ever aware of your presence, heard and received the promise that through her your Son was to be born into the world,

People: So may we live in preparation for the coming of your Son to do your holy will.

Minister: As the messenger, John the Baptist, preached repentance to prepare the way of the Lord,

People: So may we live in preparation for the coming of your Kingdom.

Minister: As the ever-watchful shepherds saw the glory in the skies,

People: May, we, too, become mindful of your glories.

Minister: As the Wise Men were guided by the Star of Peace,

People: So may the blessed Spirit always guide us and lead us into the ways of peace.

Minister: As they brought their gifts of gold, frankincense, and myrrh,

People: So may we offer ourselves and our substance.

Unison: May the message of the Heavenly Host, "Peace on earth, good will toward men," ever find echo in our hearts, and be practiced in our lives. Amen.

Baptismal Affirmation

We celebrate the baptism today of ----- and ----.

We acknowledge their desire to follow Christ as Lord of their lives.

We know they will need guidance and support in their Christian journey.

We will support them with our prayers, encouragement, and love with God's help.

LITANIES

A Litany For The New Year

Leader: Last year is behind us and we look now to the year before us.

People: We acknowledge sins, mistakes, uncompleted tasks, and hopes not realized.

Leader: Forgive us for past undoing's and give us faith and courage to move forward with confidence in the new year before us.

People: We affirm our need for the presence and guidance of Christ as we journey into the new year.

Leader: May we be alert to the needs around us and our responsibility to reach out to help the needy, ill, troubled, and any who have genuine calamities.

People: Help us to be the instruments in Christ's service for these people.

Unison: Give us guidance and strength to go into this new year with the desire to be Christlike in our personal lives and in our relationship with others.

A Litany Of Good Will

Leader: The Church declares boldly that God is the Creator of all persons.

People: We thank God for our Creator's divine love and grace.

Leader: We acknowledge, however, that racism has a long history in our world.

People: Forgive us, O God, when we have allowed prejudice to determine our relationship with other persons.

Leader: May Jesus Christ help us to break down all racial barriers and enable us to love all persons as Christ accepts and loves us.

People: May we be bridge-builders to witness to Christ's transcending love that crosses all barriers, persons, sexes, and races.

Unison: As God welcomes all persons with divine love, grant that we will work for racial harmony and good will toward all persons. Amen.

A Litany On The Cross

Leader: The Apostle Paul put the cross at the center of his preaching.

People: This was to remind us of the cost of our sins and the extent of God's love for us.

Leader: Jesus reminded his disciples on numerous occasions that he would lay down his life for them.

People: They struggled to understand why that would happen.

Leader: He also told his disciples that if anyone would follow him, they must take up their cross and follow him.

Leader: Jesus told his disciples that following him was not an easy path.

People: Forgive us, Lord, for ignoring your call to the cross-like way and seeking instead a comfortable and easy path.

Unison: We acknowledge the costly nature of our redemption by Christ's death on the cross, and the summons, as his disciples, to follow him in sacrificial service.

A Litany Of Easter

(In unison)

This is the good news which we have received, in which we stand, and by which we are saved, that Christ died for our sins according to the Scriptures, that He was buried, that He was raised on the third day, and that He appeared, first to Mary, then to Peter, and to the twelve, and then to many faithful witnesses. We believe that Jesus is the Christ, the Son of the living God. Jesus Christ is the first and the last, the beginning and the end. He is our Lord and our God. Amen.

8.

PRAYERS FOR A WEDDING

A WEDDING DINNER PRAYER

As John and Mary have consecrated their covenant of marriage, bless them now with abiding love. May their love for each other continue to grow through the years and bind them closer together. We thank you for the rich heritage their families have bestowed upon them. May the love that Christ has made with his Church bind them together into your family of love. Grace our table now with your presence as we express our thanks for this food that will nourish our bodies. Through Christ, our Lord, we pray. Amen.

PRAYER OF BLESSING

Father God, who, out of boundless love, gave us the gift of life, bless Angela and Bill, who this day pledge their love to each other. May the excitement and joy of this moment remind them of the great adventure of love which lies before them. May the love which they have received from their families assure them of the wonder of the family they begin this day. In humility we bow before the mystery of your presence in this glad hour. Amen.

A WEDDING BENEDICTION AND BLESSING

The God, who has created life, bless you with long life.

The God, who taught us how to love, inspire your love for each other.

The God, who guides the stars in their orbits, direct your path.

The God, who is the author of joy, enrich you with much happiness.

May God be in your coming in and in your going out, both now and for evermore.

Amen.

www.ingramcontent.com/pod-product-compliance
Lightning Source LLC
Chambersburg PA
CBHW031958080426
42735CB00007B/435